Performance
Addiction

Performance Addiction

The Dangerous New Syndrome and How to Stop It from Ruining Your Life

ARTHUR P. CIARAMICOLI, Ed.D., Ph.D.

WILEY

John Wiley & Sons, Inc.

Permission for quoted material on pp. 83, 84, and 92–93 granted by Random House, Inc.; from *A General Theory of Love*, by Thomas Lewis, Fari Amini, and Richard Lannon, copyright 2000. Permission for quoted material on pp. 158–159 granted by Oxford University Press; from *Calm Energy: How People Regulate Mood with Food and Exercise*, by Robert E. Thayer, copyright 2001.

Published by John Wiley & Sons, Inc., Hoboken, New Jersey
Published simultaneously in Canada

Design and composition by Navta Associates, Inc.

For general information about our other products and services, please contact our Customer Care Department within the United States at (800) 762-2974, outside the United States at (317) 572-3993 or fax (317) 572-4002.

Wiley also publishes its books in a variety of electronic formats. Some content that appears in print may not be available in electronic books. For more information about Wiley products, visit our web site at www.wiley.com.

Library of Congress Cataloging-in-Publication Data

Ciaramicoli, Arthur P.
   Performance addiction : the dangerous new syndrome and how to stop it from ruining your life / Arthur Ciaramicoli.
      p. cm.
   Includes bibliographical references and index.
   ISBN 0-471-47119-4
   1. Perfectionism (Personality trait) I. Title.
BF698.35.P47C53   2004
155.2′32—dc22

2004005663

Printed in the United States of America

10 9 8 7 6 5 4 3 2 1

To the members of Group:
If only the world had your courage, honesty, and integrity.

Contents

We are prone to judge success by the idea of our salaries or the size of our automobiles rather than by the quality of our service and relationship to mankind.

—MARTIN LUTHER KING JR.

Acknowledgments

The heart of this book is a testament to the power and value of relationships. I have been extremely fortunate to have the support and love of family and friends throughout my career, especially as this book has taken form.

My wife, Karen, has always had unyielding faith in my work as well as providing the encouragement, love, and sustenance our family needs to remain balanced. Your insightful suggestions have improved the text, and I am grateful for your patience and willingness to give me up for a while. You have always known that the door to love and respect opens when you commit to family and friends. Thank you once again for remaining loyal and true.

The greatest title I have earned in my life is being called "Dad." Our daughter Erica is the family member who lightens up the house and reminds us all to have fun. Watching you dance, sing, and enjoy life reminds me that joy is a critical ingredient in a healthy life. Your keen sense of humor always makes a difficult day disappear. Our daughter Alaina's warmth and loyalty to family lifts my spirits on a daily basis. I deeply appreciate the interest you take in my work, the many long conversations we've had about performance addiction, and I am especially thankful for your research assistance in "The Lure of Glamour" chapter. You both have unique gifts to give to the world of psychology, and I am so proud to be your father.

To my writer, collaborator, and friend, Ed Claflin. I thank God for the day our agent, Jane Dystel, suggested we work together. Your many years as an editor, author, and writer are woven into each page of this book. Your insight, intelligence, and amazing ability to make stories come to life is exceptional. Moreover, your gentle guidance and amiable personality make the process painless. I hope this is the beginning of a long writing partnership.

To my literary agent, Jane Dystel. Your support, tenacity, and wisdom are deeply appreciated. Your knowledge of the publishing world is unmatched, as is your energy for the work. I thank you for your faith in the premise of this book from the early proposal stages to the final manuscript. Your veteran expertise has been the backbone of the project.

To Jane's partner, Miriam Goderich, our thanks for your valuable contributions to the book proposal. We have proven that Yankee and Red Sox fans can unite.

To Tom Miller, executive editor, John Wiley & Sons. Your recommendations made significant improvements in the manuscript, and I am most appreciative. You provided a perspective that clarified important concepts and made the book more readable. Your advice to include workbook sections truly made this text a working, doing experience, rather than a passive reading experience. I thank Lisa Burstiner and Devra K. Nelson, senior production editors, and copy editor Mary Dorian for their meticulous review of the manuscript.

I am very thankful for my family and friends who support me throughout each writing endeavor, especially in the last few years as this book took shape. My gratitude to Janice and Jimmy Blackler, Mary and Phil Ciaramicoli, Doreen and Bryan Constantino, Ann and Doc DiVittorio, Olga and Frank DiVittorio, Jeanne and Mark Fitzpatrick, Lisa Guglielmi, Joanne and Drew Nastri, Gerry, Richard, and Pat Tessicini, Linda and Ken Thompson, Diane and Richard Werner, and Donna and Philip Wood.

A warm thank-you to my favorite young people, Kelsey and Michala Fitzpatrick. You make every day in New England sunny.

To my parents, Camie and Arthur Sr. You have not "passed away"; you have gone within. Thank you for teaching me what true love means. I share your wisdom with others every day.

A note of thanks to my colleagues and friends: Bob Cherney, Ph.D, and his wife, Mary Ellen; Valerie Sawyer-Smith, Ed.D.; and Peter Smith, Ed.D. A special thanks to my Harvard colleagues:

Richard Kadison, M.D., director of Health Services, and Tim O'Farrell, Ph.D., chief, Harvard Families and Addiction Program. Thank you to my longtime friend and spiritual adviser, Reverend Richard Fleck.

Most important, I want to thank all my clients who have allowed me to take part in their journey toward greater health. I am especially grateful to the members in my group programs. You have been my teachers. Take pride in your courageous quest for balance and peace.

Performance Addiction

Introduction

The Curse of the Capable

EARLY IN MY CLINICAL RESEARCH on the elusive problem of performance addiction, I mentioned to a colleague that I thought it might
well be the curse of the capable. His response was immediate. "If
you start a club, I'm in!" From time to time, during the ensuing years
as I've worked with people who have performance addiction, he has
continued to call it the curse of the capable, with an obvious note
of self-recognition.

In some respects it certainly is an apt description. Like a curse,
performance addiction is culturally based. Like a curse, it can be
passed from generation to generation. And like a curse, performance
addiction alters the way we regard people—particularly authority figures—lending them powers that are more mythical than human.

As for the capable part, that definitely describes most of my
clients. My first recognition of performance addiction came about
largely as a result of my work with a group of individuals who—like
many I describe in this book—embodied so many of the qualities that
are highly regarded in professional and public life. Not only did they
have mastery over practical skills, they demonstrated attitudes and
abilities that distinguished them as extraordinarily competent. But

1

when I began meeting with these people as a group, week after week, I noticed that despite their marked capabilities, they seemed to downgrade their personal achievements and physical appearance. They all seemed to be scoreboard watchers. Every day, they took inventory of how well or how terribly they were performing, how attractive or dreadful they looked in the mirror. The men seemed particularly preoccupied with money, achieving more status, and acquiring more prestigious positions. Many of the women were so self-conscious about appearance that their looks seemed to be their ticket to potential happiness. As for the men and women who transcended gender lines, the toll of performance addiction was even more exacting—the woman who not only wanted to be beautiful but also to excel in business, the man driven to become president of his company and who was equally obsessed with his physical appearance.

I started to ask myself how it was that these people did *not* see their level of capability. Whether it was the dedicated housewife, the perfectionistic schoolteacher, the self-made entrepreneur, the talented musician, or the brainy researcher, they all seemed to grossly underestimate their capabilities—that is, they caught momentary glimpses of their own value, but the perceptions were fleeting. It was as if nothing ever earned them a feeling of lasting worth. They felt compelled to prove something every day, and the task itself was devoid of emotional reward. As one of my clients put it, reciting a mantra that many knew by heart, "You're only as good as your last game, Doc."

As I continued to work with groups, it also became clear that performance addiction crosses age as well as gender barriers. In a group where the age range was late twenties to mid-thirties, performance addiction was a frequent topic of discussion. Yet the same unresolved issues were just as prominent in the group of people in their late thirties to mid-forties. My third group, comprised of people in their fifties, sixties, and seventies, was dealing with the consequences. None had been compromised in their work lives; all had achieved success. Yet in all groups, they were talking about the same affliction. Something was missing.

Whenever I asked, "What do you really want?" we would inevitably arrive at the same place. My clients would start talking about wanting to be more in control, to achieve the goals they had set for themselves, to fix their marriages, motivate their children, perfect their homes, improve their appearance. Often, the initial discussion focused on their complex and unfulfilling quests for stardom, riches, glamour, and glory. But when we looked more closely and probed more deeply, they could acknowledge a far more basic yearning for love and respect.

That is when I realized that these individuals all had their own religion. As you read further in this book and get to know the people I describe, I hope you will see just how pervasive and all-encompassing this religion can be. When we look through the eyes of true believers, we clearly see the lines drawn between good and bad, right and wrong, acceptable and unacceptable behavior. So it is with those who subscribe to the myths that underlie performance addiction. None means to do themselves or anyone else harm. In fact, those most susceptible to this particular religion are often the most capable, well intentioned, and needy.

Recently, one of my clients commented, "I thought I had all the answers, and nobody could understand why I was so driven. I had never thought of performance as an addiction." He had never felt so calm, he added, as when he came to the Friday morning group Being with others, understanding the myths behind their religion, he could clearly see the conundrum that he had dealt with for so long in isolation: "We are all driven. Everything has to be perfect, worthy of greatness. We can't slow down for fear of not being good enough."

The group had helped to lift the curse of the capable from his shoulders just as I hope this book will lift it from yours. There is no entrance exam to begin and no fifteen minutes of fame at the end. Just the possibility that you develop the skills to understand performance addiction and deal with its consequences. And as you do, I trust you will rediscover important and valuable moments of life that are most available to you with people who are nearest at hand.

1

What Is Performance Addiction?

DO YOU FEEL AS IF YOUR LIFE is in crisis? Every day, I meet people who are better educated, better paid, and better housed than their parents or grandparents were. But they are unhappy, and the unhappiness does not seem to be related to social or financial circumstances. Something else is going on.

Despite everything these people have going for them, they feel the curse of the capable. They never have enough time to do what they want to do. Their work has become a burden, the demands relentless. Worst of all, they feel removed from those who should be closest to them: family, friends, spouses, and children. And the more capable they are, the more likely they feel caught in a swirl of accelerating demands with diminishing time.

Is this happening to you? If so, why? And what can you do about it?

Are You Addicted to Performing Well?

Quite simply, performance addiction is the belief that perfecting your appearance and achieving status will secure love and respect from others. Now, I doubt that any of us are completely immune from this belief. Consciously or unconsciously, most of us have been led to think that excellent performance is a sure pathway to love and respect. This perception of the world and its rewards has been taught to us in our families and reinforced by our culture. But is it the *only* way? And will excellent performance really get us what we're after?

During some twenty-five years as a clinical psychologist, teacher, and commentator, I have been in a unique position to observe the many dimensions of performance addiction and its effect on young and old alike. I have worked with undergraduates and graduate students from Boston's most prestigious universities. I've found that people almost automatically assume that Harvard, Massachusetts Institute of Technology, and Boston College students —surely the models of outstanding achievement and excellent performance—are reveling in their personal success, confident of their futures. The reality is far different. Many of these students are deeply oppressed by the extraordinarily high expectations that have been placed on them and anguished by feelings of inadequacy. They feel dissatisfied with the fruits of their accomplishments. Many are alienated from parents and peers. Often, to my dismay, I see that patterns of addictive behavior are already well established.

My professional life as a clinical psychologist affords me another view, as well, as I treat a wide range of patients in the Boston area, from high school students to adults of all ages. As a consulting psychologist and a private clinician in a Boston suburb, I have clients who include teachers, nurses, social workers, construction workers, landscapers, college students, high school athletes, mothers, accountants, speech therapists, middle managers, engineers, salespeople, retirees, technical writers, ministers, priests, nuns, rabbis, store managers, musicians, models, radio hosts, human resource personnel, and guidance counselors, as well as CEOs, lawyers, and investment bankers.

I emphasize the diversity of this clientele because of what I have learned from them about the cross-cultural aspects of performance addiction. It's not a belief system limited to rich individuals at the pinnacle of their careers. No matter what your background, upbringing, or vocation, you may be suffering from performance addiction right now. If you have ever achieved a goal without feeling fulfilled, or have ever felt as if you just weren't good enough or doing well enough, it's probably not your career or bank account that's failing you. More likely, it's your belief system.

Have you ever thought to yourself, *I will be loved or respected if . . . ?* Everything that comes after that *if* is performance addiction. Once that belief system is fixed in your consciousness, actions become almost formulaic. To fulfill your deepest needs, you begin to think you must act better and achieve more. Feeling that others are measuring you by your deeds and accomplishments, you begin to measure your self-worth by the same standards, and wish that you could be more perfect. This is an impossibly false hope. If you buy into that wish, you become addicted to performing well. Then when good performance does not buy you happiness, you think you must perform even better. And when that, too, fails to deliver the psychic reward you seek, you decide you must try harder, go faster, be more dedicated, and make more sacrifices. That is the nature of addiction.

Performance addiction is insatiable. Don't think it can be satisfied if you make a certain amount of money, achieve great goals, or even become famous. It's not possible.

If you have performance addiction, you can't even give *yourself* permission to do an average job. It's just no longer an option. All the pressure is on being exceptional, extraordinary, and remarkable. The trouble is, if you can't give yourself permission to be average, be yourself, or do as well as you can, pretty soon the expectations set by *others* become the measure of your worth.

What Is the Source of Performance Addiction?

In this book, I'll help you discover the source or sources of performance addiction. But to do so, you need to return to the scene of the crime—where you first started to believe that you could buy love and respect by performing well. For many, the scene of the crime can be traced to an unyielding parent who demanded perfection in exchange for affection. But parental influence is only part of the picture. Another factor is the deep impact of cultural expectations.

Early in our development, most of us get a clear image of what it means to be successful. We learn that shame and guilt are attached to failure. What about the teacher who said you weren't living up to your potential? The group that snubbed you? The club that turned you down? In each of these situations, there's a clear message: Be *more* than you are, and maybe you'll be *acceptable*.

If I remind you of the scene of the crime, it's not to help stir evil memories or to settle old scores. I'd like you to view what occurred *back then* with a different set of eyes. Can you understand what happened? If you can revisit the scene and see it clearly, then you can decide for yourself whether you accept the implied promise. (That promise was: "Excel and you will be loved!") Or you can see the falsehood in that promise, which will free you from the obligation to excel and help you find your own ways to accept love and give it.

Take the Performance Addiction Quiz

Clearly, the search doesn't end with discovering the source of performance addiction. The next step is to deal with it. In this book, you'll find many examples of men and women who have come to terms with performance addiction by challenging the false formula of achievement equals love. But before you read further, here are questions that will help you find out whether you have performance addiction, and, if so, how severe it is. Only yes or no answers are required. Give the first response that comes to your mind. A simple scoring mechanism follows this quiz to help you evaluate your answers.

THE PERFORMANCE ADDICTION QUIZ

1. Did you seldom feel listened to as a child?

2. Did you worry that if you didn't please your parents you would lose their love?

3. Did you question whether your parents truly loved each other?

4. Did you often feel guilty?

5. Did you seldom have fun with your parents outside of achievement-oriented situations?

6. Were your parents quite conscious of your physical appearance?

7. Did you experience one or both parents as critical people in general?

8. Do you have memories of specific childhood hurts that have never left you?

9. Were you easily humiliated as a young person?

10. Were you considered to be a very sensitive child?

11. Do you believe your past mistakes make you unlovable today?

12. Do you want unconditional acceptance, with no criticism?

13. Do you feel irritated when people close to you are not being capable and efficient?

14. Do you always have a to-do list in your mind or in your pocket?

15. Have you considered or have you already had cosmetic surgery?

16. Are you chronically dissatisfied with the way people respond to you?

17. Do you often feel you have to work much harder than others to excel?

18. Do you wonder if anyone really loves anyone else for *who they are* rather than for *what they do*?

19. Are you frequently trying to perfect the way you speak?

20. Are you frequently trying to perfect your appearance?

21. Do you often discover that people are far less critical than you imagined?

22. Do you have trouble tolerating your own imperfections?

23. Do you have trouble tolerating others' imperfections?

24. Do you often wonder how much money others make?

25. When friends, relatives, or colleagues have success, do you feel you don't measure up?

26. Are you unable to stop perfectionist thinking even though you know it's irrational?

27. Are you afraid that if you were not so driven you would be lazy?

28. Do you feel guilty if you just hang out and do nothing?

29. Are you afraid of trying to learn new things for fear of being humiliated?

30. Deep down, do you think you're "not much"?

31. No matter what you think *of* yourself, do you find that you can't stop thinking *about* yourself?

32. Does your self-voice tend to be punitive rather than understanding?

33. Do you tend to generalize about yourself in a negative way under stress? (Do you say things to yourself like "I'm so stupid!" or "I'm so fat!"?)

34. Are you seldom content to be with one person in one place for very long?

35. Are you easily bored in conversation?

36. Does your energy pick up when the conversation is about you?

37. Do you like being idealized by others?

38. Do you tend to idealize others?

39. Do you feel pressured to impress others in order to secure their love?

40. Do you fear that loss of status will lead to loss of love?

41. Are you afraid you don't know what true love really is?

42. Have you seldom felt loved the way you want to be loved?

43. Is it difficult for you to truly trust others?

44. Do you question whether you have true friends?

45. Are you afraid your long-term love relationship is based on what you do for each other rather than a deeper sense of love?

46. Do you have sexual relations infrequently?

47. Are you seldom "present in the moment" during sex?

48. Do you weigh yourself daily?

49. Are you intolerant of weight gain?

50. Are you intolerant of the aging process?

51. Do you imagine if you could perfect certain body parts your life would be dramatically improved?

52. Do you compare your financial situation to others?

53. Do you notice the cars people drive and rate those people accordingly?

54. Do you feel uncomfortable and less worthy in a home that is larger and more extravagant than your own?

55. Do have a sense of inferiority in relation to people who have more education than you?

56. Do you tend to attach certain personality characteristics to those who attended prestigious schools?

57. Do you rank people according to the affluence of the town or city where they live?

58. Do you feel deprived when a neighbor or friend has a more attractive spouse than yours?

59. Do you fantasize about being with someone who is far more attractive than your spouse or lover?

60. Do you think that if you were more attractive you would be with a different spouse or lover?

61. Do you think that if you were more successful financially you would be with a different spouse or lover?

62. Do you tend to think that others have had an unfair advantage in terms of the success they have achieved?

63. Do you measure another person's success apart from the quality of that person's relationships?

64. Do you measure success without giving much weight to a person's character?

65. Assuming that you know how to care for your body, do you find that you are seldom consistent with your self-care measures?

66. Do you exercise too little or too much?

67. Are you on a diet at least once every year?

68. At least once a week, do you have three or more alcoholic drinks in a single day?

69. Do you take sleep aids monthly or more often?

70. Do you consider exercise and proper sleep and nutritional habits low priorities in your life?

71. Do you drink more than three caffeinated beverages per day?

72. Do you often eat comfort foods, especially in the evening?

73. Do you seldom think about the quality of your relationships?

74. With each passing year, do you think you become less desirable to others?

To score this quiz, add one point for every yes answer. Add up the total number of points, and use the following to rate the level of your performance addiction:

Score (yes answers)	Your level of performance addiction
60+	Severe
50–59	Significant
40–49	Moderate
30–39	Mild
20–29	Low

No matter what the level of your addiction, you will find useful questions and self-evaluations in this book. There are questions to ask yourself, recommendations for what you can do, and exercises that will help guide you through an exploration of performance addiction. Using these specific guidelines, you can trace the origins of the beliefs that cause some level of performance addiction in your behavior. And you can use the exercises to help replace those beliefs with a more balanced life.

In addition, I'll let you be a fly on the wall so that you can listen to intimate discussions I've had with people at all levels of performance addiction. While I have, of course, altered names and some details of my clients to preserve anonymity, the dilemmas they face are unchanged. I hope that by sharing their stories, I will help you come to your own conclusions about the origins of your own performance addiction.

As you free yourself from the unconscious control of performance addiction, you will find yourself with greater energy. You don't need to focus on idealized outcomes or constantly direct your energy toward elusive success. As you overcome performance addiction, you'll discover new meaning in your work and relationships to help you go beyond material reward. You'll find out how work can become a true expression of your sense of self and how relationships can be valued in terms of love and friendship rather than status and image.

Far too many of us are just enduring the curse of the capable, rather than addressing the performance addiction at the root of this malaise. But trying to ignore performance addiction can cost you dearly, particularly in terms of failed relationships. This book can help you lift the curse, address your performance addiction, and come away with a true sense of the wonderful rewards you can get from the ordinary things in your life.

2

Performance Addiction in Your Life

DURING MORE THAN TWENTY-FIVE years of working with many kinds of addicts, I have learned that all addictions represent an attempt to avoid or quickly resolve some level of conflict. The addictive behavior reinforces a lack of faith in oneself: "I can't deal with this! I need a drink (or a cigarette, a sex partner, a big win, etc.)."

Performance addiction is like a lot of other addictions that you already know about. The drive to perform, rate your performance, and watch the scoreboard every day gives you the illusion that if you just keep going, you can protect yourself from real anxiety and conflict. So, if you have performance addiction, you turn to activity the same way alcoholics reach for a drink or gamblers turn to the gaming table. It's a way of not dealing with anxiety. It helps avoid conflict. ("Sorry . . . can't talk now! Got a million things to do!")

But it's more than avoidance. If you have performance addiction, I'll bet you have the tendency to idealize others. You probably figure that those who are performing, achieving, and perfecting feel more worthwhile than you do. Looking at them, it's easy to imagine that they have achieved happiness. And if you can just work a little harder, maybe you can, too. That's where the illusion comes in. In the case of Rachel, one of my clients, the illusion that she could work and perfect herself into a state of happiness took over her whole life.

RACHEL: THE CONSULTANT WHO HIDES HER ANXIETY

Rachel is a forty-two-year-old tax consultant who specializes in mergers and takeovers. She appears to have always known what she wanted and how to get it. She is making a top salary with one of Boston's leading accounting firms, earning more than she ever anticipated.

Rachel told me that she chose her profession "because I knew people would respect me." And why shouldn't they? She is a smart, accomplished, and attractive professional at the pinnacle of her career.

But there's another Rachel quite different from the one who performs so well in the corporate environment. The unseen Rachel has massive anxiety, though she uses humor to hide it. In her office she's great at telling jokes and making side comments that keep people in stitches. But every once in a while her behavior gets out of control. People are still talking about last year's holiday party when she drank too much and hopped on a table to imitate Tina Turner. Her boss, who is a principal partner in the firm, told her to clean up her act. "Our clients were there!" he reminded her. "Do you think they'll want you to represent them if you act like that?"

Now Rachel avoids office parties. She fears if she doesn't drink, she'll be a bore. But if she does, she'll get out of line. She worries constantly about how she appears. Will other people see her insecurity? Will she finally do something utterly unforgivable?

Rachel *always* feels the pressure to perform. That's how she got through business school, which she hated. Nothing was easy for her, and she didn't feel that she belonged in one of the nation's top MBA programs. To Rachel it seemed like the other students knew what they were doing. Not her. Not ever. She studied to the point of exhaustion. Even when she finally got her graduate degree, she didn't feel like she deserved it. She passed the CPA exam, but felt as though she just barely got through.

With Rachel there is always more that she feels she must do. "Look at this!" she exclaims, trying to pinch rolls of fat from her stomach. "I look like I'm pregnant!" Far from it, I could tell her, but she is obsessed with her appearance. She frequently talks about her "short legs." Last year, she had an eye lift and cheek implants. Unfortunately, the implants were too large for her face, soon causing an infection; they had to be removed, and they left an indentation on both sides of her face. She is currently seeking another cosmetic surgeon to try to repair the damage.

She gets up at 5:30 every morning to work out on a treadmill. She lifts weights and meets with a personal trainer twice a week—not that she takes joy in exercising. It's just to wage war on her "fat."

Rachel has been in and out of relationships. "I've given up looking for Mr. Right," she tells me. "I'm looking for Mr. *Right Now*." Currently, Mr. Right Now is a married man she met at a bar. "I know I should feel guilty," she says, "but I am starving for affection. Guys like him never pick up women like me for real. So I pretend he loves me, and he acts like it, but I still end up sleeping alone."

Actually, Rachel has one constant companion. It is the voice that tells her to be more capable, successful, confident, and attractive. She responds to that voice without knowing why. Despite her excellent reputation with the firm, she has steadily taken on more clients and volunteered to travel anywhere in the country to secure more business. No matter how good she looks, she thinks she must try to look better. Above all, she feels compelled to hide her real identity behind the mask of performance.

On the drive to work, her thoughts race ahead. "I seldom remember the drive," she tells me. "I am so focused on what's going to happen when I get to the office."

Rachel should be able to look back with pride on her years of success. She should feel confident that she can meet the demands of each new day. Instead, she is plagued with worry. No matter how well she prepares, there is always more to accomplish and something unfinished. Rachel never feels capable of performing well enough.

Some years ago, Rachel had the illusion that accomplishment would make up for everything else that was missing in her life. Things are not turning out that way. "Let's face it, I am always going to be alone," Rachel says. "I am a struggling corporate executive—great title, great money, empty heart."

It's a powerful admission but perhaps a new beginning. Rachel has come to recognize that her anxiety and uneasiness are rooted in performance addiction.

What Are Your Signs of Performance Addiction?

If you've taken the quiz in chapter 1, I'm sure you've already recognized some similarities between Rachel's symptoms of performance addiction and your own. Perhaps you chose your work or profession with the expectation that it would earn you respect. Or you feel the daily obligation of turning in a performance that requires you to hide your anxiety. Or you're so focused on looking better and working harder that you can't remember the last time you were able to really relax and be yourself.

It's no news that addiction takes many forms—from alcoholism and gambling to sex addiction and eating disorders. Each of these has its unique set of dynamics. Although varied, addictive behaviors are united by a common theme that "life will be beautiful once I'm in recovery."

People with addictions are prone to idealize others. The myth perpetuated through years of addictive behavior is that "when I give this up, I will have everything, just like other people have."

Of course, it hardly ever happens that way. Suppose you have an addiction that you give up tomorrow. Then you find out your life doesn't change that much! You don't feel deliriously happy with the transformation. In fact, in some ways you feel the same as you did before. Then the question becomes: "Now that I have given up drinking (or bingeing, or gambling, or having affairs), why is my life so lousy? What's the point if all I'm going to feel is anxious and depressed?"

People with addictions get accustomed to substituting superficial means of achieving happiness. When they no longer have the addictive behavior to take the edge off, they feel anxious. They may not be able to maintain an internal structure to manage everyday tensions.

In *Willpower Is Not Enough: Recovery from Addiction of Every Kind*, Arnold M. Washton and Donna Boundy observe that the person at high risk for addiction "suffers from a gnawing sense of loneliness deep within." The addictive personality is likely to feel out of touch with others and out of touch with himself or herself.

"The addict is often as preoccupied with his drug as a lover is with the object of his dreams," according to Washton and Boundy. "He may seem to love, honor, and protect the supply of his drug more than he does the people in his household. That's because the drug provides feelings of connectedness with others—without the demands of real intimacy."

If we substitute the word *performance* for *drug*, this is an almost perfect description of how people talk about their performance addiction. Love is the objective. But if you have performance addiction, winning that love is likely to be a lot of work. That's because you have the illusion that increased activity and achievement will get you what you want. It is a grand, misdirected project.

Where Did Your Performance Addiction Start?

If you look around you and listen to what people are talking about, my guess is that you'll find a lot of evidence of performance addiction. Indeed, if you have it, you're certainly not alone. But why is it so common? Where does it all start? And why do we have so much trouble recognizing performance addiction for what it is?

In my clinical work with groups and individuals, I began to see evidence of performance addiction long before I had a name for it. Interacting with people from a wide variety of cultural, racial, and religious backgrounds, it was hard for me to see what their histories had in common.

Yet when these people got together in therapy groups and discussed common issues, many described a sense of discontent that others found immediately familiar. Many had reached a point in their lives where they certainly had material success. Yet they spoke as if true rewards were still out of reach. Most appeared successful in their professions—some, extremely so. Many were fit and attractive. But their internal view of themselves did not match their achievements. They were dissatisfied with how they appeared to others.

What was overshadowing lives that wore all the bright banners of success, affluence, attractiveness, and accomplishment?

They seemed disappointed. But why? Clearly, they had expectations about themselves, their world, and the rewards they deserved. Why weren't they enjoying their success? Why weren't they taking pleasure in their accomplishments? Instead, they seemed to be almost frantically seeking reassurance that they were still on the right track.

Did they really have it all but just couldn't see it? Or was there something false in the implicit promises they had been given—often, from childhood forward—about excellent performance leading to incomparable rewards?

I realized that for many of my clients, their discontent was rooted in childhood experiences. If we wanted to figure out their emptiness, we had to go back to the scene of the crime.

Clues from the Scene of the Crime

Rachel has more than the simmering anxieties of a woman who cannot find peace with herself. She has a need to find meaning. And in the past that need has been met by working on her goals. Like anyone with an addiction, she has established a pattern that is very hard to break.

Yet Rachel's success has been accompanied by a dismaying sense of loneliness and isolation. She was married to a handsome stock broker. The man had left his wife to marry Rachel, then ultimately repeated his extramarital behavior in their relationship. When she confronted him with evidence of his infidelities, he vowed to be faithful, but he could not keep his promise and they divorced.

When he left, Rachel fell into a deep depression. She drank too much and worked more and more hours. She eventually had an affair with one of her prominent clients. Known for being a playboy, he had walked out of his first marriage and was about to dissolve his second. Rachel had known all about him before their affair began. Though he fit her image of the man she thought she should be with, Rachel had assumed all along that there was little chance of lasting intimacy.

As this relationship also came to an end, Rachel resumed the overdrive mode that is the current pattern of her daily life—getting up earlier, working harder, and putting in hours of exercise to perfect her physique. This is what she has always done. Both figuratively and literally, she is running faster and faster, with the devotion of a true addict. But all the additional activity and hard work have not satisfied the hunger she feels.

This pattern really started in her childhood, back at the scene of the crime. As she revisited that scene, she realized how the groundwork had been laid for an addiction that had nothing to do with alcohol or drugs. For her, the alluring "substance" was an ever-elusive ideal of performance.

Rachel is the second youngest in a family of five. Her three older brothers are all very successful. Her baby sister has Down syndrome and was clearly her mother's favorite. As Rachel describes her mother, I get the picture of a woman who was never good enough for her husband or accepted by her husband's side of the family. His family was affluent and highly educated; her blue-collar family was always struggling financially. Rachel represented the female who might turn out to be just what everyone wanted—the bright, ambitious, and beautiful young woman who would make up for her mother's deficiencies.

In Rachel's home the struggle for acceptance focused first on her appearance. Her brothers had made fun of Rachel's chubby figure when she was a child. When she reached adolescence and realized she was sexually attractive to boys, her sexuality became a point of contention with her mother.

"My mother seemed asexual," Rachel says. "I think the word *sex* made her perspire. I finally had something she didn't. I was saying, 'You hate me, but I am more of a woman than you can ever be.'"

The fight to prove herself has been never-ending for Rachel. It was a key factor in her career choice as an accountant specializing in mergers and takeovers. "I think I was attracted to the corporate world to be hard," she tells me. "I try to fill that role. I am a tough negotiator. I know how to manipulate and influence clients, but I know now that my drive to influence comes from my lifelong feelings of helplessness. I want to change how I felt as a kid, I want to feel powerful. I don't think I can ever soften up to let anyone close."

And so the pattern was established. All along, Rachel behaved in a way that would let her prove herself, setting her apart from others as a paradigm of attractiveness, sexuality, professional achievement, and affluence. All those goals were achieved. Now she wants more. But working harder, achieving more, and perfecting her physical appearance are not helping her attain the attachment to others that is at the core of her search.

In Rachel's professional and personal life, she tells me, she has come to know people who have suffered far more. Yet some of them, she says, seem to grow and go on to form richer relationships than she ever dreamed of. "I have all the wealth," she observes, "yet

I have become impossible to be around. I feel so cheated, so jaded. I am a bitter success."

Upward Mobility, Inward Conflict

What did your parents expect of you? What did they want you to become? How did they get across that message to you? If you can answer these questions, you'll get a good glimpse of the scene of the crime.

We'll explore some of these scenes in chapter 4. But first consider how your family set the stage for performance addiction. I think we can agree that achievement and prosperity—the dual symbols of getting ahead—are central to the fabric of American life. Even if upward mobility seems out of reach to many people, it's still something that generations of Americans believe in. The parents who lived through the Depression and World War II wanted their children to focus on hard work, higher education, and affluence. Children are supposed to build on their parents' success or make up for lost opportunities. It's likely you got a strong message from your own grandparents and parents that achievement would lead to prosperity and fulfillment.

I can bear witness to that experience in my own family. My father served with distinction in the OSS (the forerunner of the CIA) during World War II. Afterward, he ran a very successful furniture store—a demanding and time-consuming business that he pursued with tremendous determination. One day, some two years after I had received my doctorate and started my practice, my father dropped by for a Saturday morning visit.

My wife and I had just had our first child, Erica, and I was having a great time playing with her. While my father was there, I got a phone call from a very respected physician who asked whether I would see one of his patients. When I told the physician that my practice was full, he tried to cajole me a bit, but I knew I simply did not have time for any more patients. Politely but decisively I said that there was no way I could increase my caseload.

When I hung up the phone, I realized my father had overheard the entire conversation. He was livid. He could not believe that someone who was just starting out would "refuse a referral and reject the opportunity to work." I told him that if I saw this patient, it would mean working on Saturday, and I didn't want to give up the time with Erica. To my father, that was just an excuse. We had words, and he left angrily.

I felt awful. And I felt guilty. Clearly, my dad thought I was not a hard worker and that I lacked perseverance.

Several years later, my dad came to visit us. Again it was on a Saturday. My mother had died of breast cancer, and he was lost without her. He was retired. Not working long hours, as he had always done, he didn't seem to know what to do with himself.

When he arrived this time, I was seeing a patient in my home office—one of two sessions I had scheduled that day. Between sessions, I came downstairs to find my father playing with our two girls.

After I had finished up the session with my second client, my father and I had coffee and chatted for a while. As he approached the door to leave, he mentioned that he wanted to talk with me.

When my dad made this kind of request, I knew something was really important to him. He had become much more expressive after my mother's death.

As we walked to the car, he told me how much he loved me, then went on to say that I needed to put my life in perspective. "You are working to help people and make a living, but the most important part of your life is in front of you—and you're missing the boat. Those girls are worth millions. I wish I could do it over again. I would spend every minute with you and your brother. Don't make work your god. Nothing is as important as your wife and children."

He told me that he knew I would see the way. Then he got in his car, gave me the V sign (as he always did), and drove off.

That night, my wife and I were out with friends when I received a call. I was told that my father had been stricken with a massive heart attack. He died before he reached the hospital.

My dad's initial lesson was to work all you can and never say no to anyone. When he lost my mother and contemplated the course of his own life, he began to see things from a different perspective.

Unfortunately, many from the post–World War II generation got only the first message from their parents and never the second. The work ethic was communicated in the form of conditional love—that is, "If you work hard and persevere, you will have my respect and affection."

How Perfect Do You Need to Be?

If you have long felt that being successful and living up to your potential are part of your birthright, you may also be aware of your own tendency to try to make things perfect. In fact, perfectionism and performance addiction often go hand in hand.

In recent years, there have been many studies on the qualities of the perfectionistic personality. We're beginning to get insight into the way perfectionism runs in families.

In 1992, a psychologist at Pennsylvania State University, Robert B. Slaney, worked with a graduate student, Doug Johnson, to develop an Almost Perfect Scale (APS) designed to measure the components of perfectionism. Initially, the scale was developed to help clinicians explain the attitudes of two students who seemed to have a puzzling array of psychological concerns. Though these students were doing well in an academic environment, both were extremely unhappy. According to Slaney, "It became clear that the students' goals or standards differed from their perceptions of their performances. The perceived difference between their standards and their performance seemed like a potentially important source of their unhappiness."

Could it be, the researchers asked, that the students' dissatisfaction with performance was related to perfectionism? And if so, how?

The authors used a revised version of the APS as an instrument in their studies. They discovered that perfectionism by itself did not contribute directly to the unhappiness or dissatisfaction of individuals. On the contrary, the authors concluded, setting high standards was crucial to a sense of worth. The individuals who did set high standards refused to lower them even a notch or two. They couldn't allow themselves. Lowering their standards would erode their self-esteem.

"The most obvious challenge," Slaney concluded, "may be to decrease the experiences of dissatisfaction, angst, or unhappiness while indicating that the maintenance of standards for performance is possible, reasonable, and even desirable. This approach seems necessary because the possession of high standards for one's performance is basic to the fabric of U.S. and Western societies and seems highly related to the reluctance of interview participants to give up their perfectionism."

Drawing on a number of other studies for comparison, Slaney suggested that a distinction should be made between adaptive and maladaptive perfectionism. "The adaptive perfectionist, who experiences less distress related to perfectionism and may be trying for high standards, may be appropriately pursuing high standards, a sign of mental health. . . . In contrast, maladaptive perfectionists may pursue high standards to avoid feelings of inferiority."

If you have a high level of performance addiction, there's a good chance you have the kind of perfectionism that's maladaptive rather than adaptive. Activity, in itself, becomes a way to make up for feelings of unworthiness. You start to believe that feelings of inferiority will be vanquished by meeting extremely high performance standards. But when you can't reach the goal—you can't be perfect—what happens? That's where the unhappiness comes in.

Did Your Parents Approve?

When we seek the connection between a high degree of perfectionism and low feelings of self-worth, parental approval looks like a big factor. Gordon L. Flett, Ph.D., from the University of

Ontario, and a number of colleagues have looked at the close connection between perfectionism in children and their parents. Central to this relationship is the concept of contingent self-worth—that is, the parent sends a message to the child that communicates "my love and approval are contingent on your successful performance."

From their studies on the social impact of perfectionism, Flett and his fellow researchers concluded, "In general, exposure to conditions that foster a sense of conditional self-worth also increases the likelihood that a state of helplessness will develop. . . . People who score high on measures of socially prescribed perfectionism and who tend to endorse such statements as, 'The better I do, the better I am expected to do,' are likely to have been exposed to conditions of contingent self-worth, and they are highly vulnerable to feelings of helplessness in response to negative feedback from others."

If you grew up in a family where performance and behavior were constantly being scrutinized, you probably figured out pretty quickly what made you acceptable. How did your parents evaluate your worthiness? As the authors of the Flett study point out, in "highly evaluative families" there are always measures of goodness and badness. There's constant scrutiny. Even material goods fall into some category on the scale from bad to good.

Growing up in this environment, you're likely to have a self-image that's as clear as the measuring tape on a door jamb. Only it's a psychic measuring tape. Praise and approbation make you taller. Failure makes you shorter. Eventually, under this influence, you develop an internal gradient. You have the ability to measure your performance on a scale from inadequate to perfect. If you internalize this gradient scale and buy into perfectionism, you're almost assured of being cut off from easy and enjoyable experiences.

About the time of my father's death, I was given a book by Hugh Prather called *Notes to Myself*. I remember only one line: "We can either be perfect or we can be human." To me this phrase summarizes the problem with perfectionism. As we get closer and closer to the state of perfection, we must go to ever-greater lengths to hide our mistakes, flaws, and shortcomings—that is, all that makes us most appealingly human.

Marrying Performance Addiction

Initially, the spouses or lovers of performance addicts are impressed by what they perceive as the character and drive of high achievers. As time goes on, the partner comes to realize the addictive aspect of the other person's desire for success and his or her dependency on achievement. So, ultimately, performance addiction causes enormous interpersonal distress.

When two people each grew up with highly perfectionistic parents and then get married, the playing out of performance addiction leads to a kind of self-evaluation and self-judgment that is almost stultifying.

RON AND MARTHA: WED TO PERFECTIONISM

Ron and Martha, two clients in marital therapy, work together in a family-owned business. He is the president; she is the office manager. For years, the business has prospered, and they are doing so well that both of them could leave the company in other hands if both were just willing to let go.

About once a year, Martha gets sick from overwork and contemplates hiring someone to help her out. On several occasions, she has given Ron the green light to recruit an assistant for her, but each time she has found something wrong with the new employee. Her most common complaint: "They don't have a work ethic." Each of her assistants has been fired within a few months.

Perfectionism drives her to work to the breaking point and beyond. Ron's perfectionism is expressed in a different way. Before they go anywhere, Ron makes detailed plans outlining each day's activities. What if anything is left to chance?

Precious vacation time could be wasted! From Martha's perspective, nobody, including the children, enjoys having vacation activities so carefully planned.

Ron and Martha are prime examples of performance-addicted personalities united in marriage. The dynamics have forced them into a stalemate. Their relationship flounders because neither is dealing with his or her perfectionism. Martha cannot fathom anyone being able to do her job as well as she does, so she won't relinquish responsibilities in the business. Ron can't let go enough to enjoy his vacation without planning it to the hilt. The family is unable to move ahead toward a more fulfilling and meaningful enjoyment of each other's presence and more life-enhancing spontaneity in their activities.

Money and Performance Addiction

Of course, we have to take money into account. Outstanding performance *is* rewarded. The very hard workers *do* get promoted. Top grades lead to top schools, which lead to top jobs and top salaries. No arguing with that.

But performing well in order to learn a subject, get into a good school, find the right job, or earn a promotion is something quite different from performance addiction. If you know what you're after, go for it, and get it, more power to you. It only becomes a problem when you believe that acing the test or landing the plum job will also win you respect and happiness. In fact, when the drive to make money becomes all-consuming, it can lead to the depths of unhappiness.

In a long-term study of college students conducted by UCLA and the American Council of Education, nearly a quarter of a million entering students were asked to name "a very important reason to go to college." In 1971, one out of two college students listed "to make more money" as the prime goal. By 1998, the ratio was three out of four. The proportion of students who considered it essential to become "very well off" rose from 39 percent in 1970 to 74 percent in 1998. Among nineteen listed objectives, being "very well off" was number one, outranking "developing a meaningful philosophy of life," "becoming an authority in my field," "helping others in difficulty," and "raising a family."

Do you have similar goals? If so, it's quite likely you're setting yourself up for disappointment—not because you won't become very well off but because *well off* refers to economics, not a state of mind.

If This Isn't the Road to Happiness, What Is?

In studies of affluent countries (defined as those countries where most people can afford life's necessities), researchers have found that affluence matters surprisingly little as a measure of happiness. In the United States, Canada, and Europe, the correlation between income and personal happiness is surprisingly weak—indeed, virtually negligible. Even the very rich are only slightly happier than the average American, judging from a survey of the Forbes 100 Richest Americans conducted by University of Illinois psychologist Ed Diener in 1985.

I think most Americans assume that they will become increasingly content as their standard of life improves. Between 1960 and 1997, by almost any objective measure of household goods and conveniences, the American standard of living increased substantially. The percentage of homes with dishwashers rose from 7 percent to 50 percent, according to the U.S. Department of Consumer Affairs. In 1950, about one-quarter of U.S. households had clothes dryers and air conditioners. By 1998, these conveniences were in nearly three-quarters of all households.

What happened to the happiness rating during these four decades of unprecedented material prosperity? Thirty-five percent of Americans rated themselves as "very happy" in 1957. Forty years later, only 33 percent said they were "very happy." During that time, the divorce rate doubled, the teen suicide rate tripled, and violent crime nearly quadrupled. The Forbes study concluded, "Our becoming much better off over the last four decades *has not been accompanied by one iota of increased subjective well-being*" (italics added).

What is missing? Why do so many people who possess so much still feel like they can't access happiness? What can be done about it?

The answer for many people is to try harder to feed the hunger. Both literally and figuratively. People who feel that their lives are empty and meaningless eat more than they need to. Some may develop addictions to alcohol, pharmaceutical and street drugs, sex, or gambling. When they cannot fill the emptiness, anxiety soars. They speed up the pace and strive to do more. They have trouble falling asleep at night, even when they are seized by exhaustion. They take pills to cure the insomnia, then other pills to stay awake.

And they become addicted to performance. "If I can only do more and do it better, maybe I'll capture the missing happiness." But of course it doesn't work that way. Performance addicts become consumed with the fear that they will be shown up as far less than perfect indeed, mediocre—if their failures and weaknesses are known.

A fascinating perspective on Western attitudes toward achievement is provided by the Sherpa mountaineer Jamling Tenzing Norgay, who was climbing leader of the 1996 IMAX expedition to the peak of Everest. The son of the first Sherpa who accompanied Sir Edmund Hillary on his famed ascent, Jamling had the opportunity to study in the United States for a number of years before returning to Katmandu. In his book, *Touching My Father's Soul*, he reflects on that experience.

As an American student, Jamling says, he began to feel as if "meaning and connection were missing from my life in the United States, as if the country were lacking a spiritual core. All momentum and no center." Looking at the urgent pace pursued by his fellow students, Jamling started to wonder what they were actually accomplishing. "Success was the universal holy grail," he reflects, "and my American classmates had begun to pursue it even before they graduated."

Jamling had come to America expecting to discover the spiritual core at the heart of the nation's dynamism. But it wasn't there. "Its absence," he observes, "is the source of restlessness, dissatisfaction, and confusion that I saw afflicting many Americans. Wealth and material possessions haven't eased their malaise. Perhaps they have only aggravated it."

To that I would add that while we are striving and achieving, relationships suffer terribly. This is the core of the dilemma: Performance addiction ultimately deprives us of relational integrity, which is the ability to place relationships with family and community above our quest for power and image. If we truly embrace relational integrity, our view of ourselves as honest and ethical human beings will not permit us to compromise our core values or make them secondary. But without relational integrity, we lose the intimacy with other human beings that we most need to get love and respect.

How Do You Cope with Performance Addiction?

For Rachel, Ron, Martha, and many other performance addicts, striving for perfection is as addictive as a drug. It is a learned pattern of coping that provides a mental vacation from self-consciousness.

If you're trying to win everything you want by increasing your level of activity, you are involved in a dizzying acceleration. In *Faster: The Acceleration of Just about Everything,* author James Gleick summarizes the characteristics of a high-paced society that is fueled by stress and stoked by ambition. "If one quality defines our modern, technological age, it is acceleration," writes Gleick. "We are making haste. Our computers, our movies, our sex lives, our prayers—they all run faster now than before. And the more we fill our lives with time-saving devices and time-saving strategies, the more rushed we feel."

Theoretically, if we're getting the benefit of time-saving devices, we should have more leisure time. In reality, the opposite has happened. We're working longer hours and taking fewer and shorter vacations than at any time since World War II. Rather than relieving stress through the avenue of hard work, stress increases as we pour more energy into activity and leave less time for ourselves.

A survey of 401 executives of U.S. organizations shows that absenteeism has gone up 2.5 percent in seven years, which is "a strong indication that stress and accompanying tension are on the rise," according to Gleick. And the acceleration is having a dramatic impact on the next generation as well. Gleick cites a study conducted by the Yale School of Medicine that suggests many young people are paying an unanticipated price. Between 1995 and 1999, the study documented a 59 percent increase in hospital admissions for depression, violence, drug ingestion, suicide attempts, and behavior changes among children ages four to fifteen.

While it may be possible to detect signs of performance addiction in others, perhaps it is not so easy to see indicators within yourself. Even if you do, you may be debating the danger. After all, you probably feel like your achievements have earned you some degree of success. If the formula seems to have worked so far, why change it?

You need to make changes if you begin to have an inkling that something is not quite right. If you start to suspect that the payoffs you've been waiting for in terms of love and respect are not there, it is time to search deeper. If you are beginning to wonder whether you're following the wrong path, you may be ready to take a closer look at things.

I think it is essential to emphasize that excellent performance, high standards of achievement, and lofty goals are not in themselves signals of performance addiction. On the contrary, optimum performance is highly desirable. But those who take real joy in their work and activities find that the process of measuring achievement by outcomes is secondary.

People who relish their work and play have an intrinsic joy in performing at high levels. But such joy is *in the moment.* Successful accomplishment does not become the exclusive measurement of self-worth. Rather, the accomplishment is more immediate. It is the *doing* rather than *the anticipation of the outcome* that serves as a measure of worthiness.

If you recognize performance addiction and deal with it, you will actually achieve at higher levels, with more joy and less stress. The feeling is the equivalent of what sports psychologists call the "flow state" or "being in the zone." John Gilmore, a psychologist who has studied the accomplishments of superior athletes, notes that when these athletes are performing at their highest level, they are having fun with no concern about past records and very little concern about the possible future outcome or nonperformance. The flow state, he observes, "is not consciously seen as a means to an end, but as an end in itself. It is so pleasurable that all one wants to do is perpetuate the experience."

It is great fun to love your work. And I believe it is possible for each one of us (not just superior athletes!) to experience the flow state, in which we are totally caught up in the pleasure of the activity of the moment. This is what it truly means to reach your potential—finding enjoyment in the process rather than focusing on the outcome. But you can reach your potential only when the drive is inherently rich, not a misdirected attempt to resolve issues of self-worth or self-esteem.

Examining the true reasons for your drive is critical. Is performance an immensely satisfying end in itself, or is it a way to prove your worth to others and to yourself? Discovering the answer to this question is important. It is a way to find meaning in your own life and in your relationships with others.

What You Can Do about Performance Addiction

- Describe ten situations, events, or occurrences that would give you all you want in life.

- Differentiate between wishes that are performance addiction–based and those that would be genuinely, intrinsically pleasurable.

- Out of those ten situations, how many are performance addiction–based?

- Describe twenty moments that have already occurred in your life that could be called universal moments of joy, such as the birth of a child, falling in love, seeing an old friend after years of absence, or a musical experience. How many of these experiences required performance-addiction satisfaction such as awards, compliments from others, earning money, or material purchases?

3

Evidence of
Performance Addiction

1. Can you engage in relaxing activities without thoughts that you are being lazy or slacking off?

2. Is there a parent or spouse whom you feel you can never please for very long?

3. Do you ever truly enjoy your work without being focused on the dollar amount of your efforts?

4. Do you strive to please authority figures such as bosses or managers without ever feeling secure about their approval?

5. Do you long for a certain kind of affection you feel you seldom receive?

6. Do you feel jealous when others accomplish great things?

7. Do you often pick out faults or imperfections in those who are close to you even when you try to be more tolerant?

8. Is it difficult for you to stay focused when a spouse, child, or coworker is speaking?

9. Do you often evaluate your appearance, intelligence, and material possessions?

I'M SURE YOU HAVE MORE than a yes or no answer for each question. These issues are very close to all of us—the way we feel about ourselves, our work, and our families; the values and accomplishments we hold dear; the ways we seek affection and search for self-esteem. In this chapter I'll introduce you to some people who have wrestled with these issues to encourage you to explore your own feelings in more depth. But first you need to ask yourself: What is success?

That's exactly the question I posed when I was the facilitator of a group discussing performance addiction. The question came up because one member had just described a very successful negotiation with a potential employer.

SUSAN: WHEN YOU CAN'T SETTLE FOR LESS

Susan has an MBA. She, her physician husband, and their daughter can live comfortably on his salary and their investments. She decided to ask for a part-time rather than a full-time job. She wanted more time for herself as well as more time to spend with her daughter and her husband. And she got everything she wanted.

So what felt wrong about her interview? Why wasn't she happy with the outcome?

Susan felt guilty. Having come so far and done so much, how could she "settle" for a part-time job? She says the uneasiness originated with her mother's expectations. In her mother's view, corporate success was everything. "My mother doesn't know what's happening. I'm a woman with an MBA—someone who has attended prestigious universities. Someone like me should be in demand. How can I just accept a part-time job? I must be letting her down."

But that's not the whole story. As we probe further, Susan touches another level of her feelings about herself. "I know my mother would accept anything I do eventually. But it just seems I've been geared this way for so long, I can't believe anything else. It's not her view of success anymore. It's mine. Success is the *only* way. Success at all costs!" This is what I call the self-voice.

Your Dictatorial Self-Voice

The voice that Susan hears is what I call a self-voice. It's an internal voice that speaks to us so constantly and with such determined consistency that we may not even be aware of it. To Susan the self-voice was saying, "Success is the only way—success at all costs!" She understood where this voice originated. It came from her mother. But how did it become such an integral part of her own internal makeup?

As a child, your sense of yourself was very much a work in progress. You had experiences with being rewarded or punished that helped to shape you. If you swore out loud and your parents looked angry and disapproving, the message probably seemed clear: "Don't swear!" But was it really so straightforward? That apparently simple message may have had many colorations depending on the nature of your parents and what they really communicated. At one extreme, it might have meant that swearing was unforgivable and you would be punished every time you did it. But another insinuation might have been that you could swear when you were with friends but not with your parents. Or your parents could swear but you couldn't. Or when you swore, you were unacceptable. So which of those underlying meanings did you most likely hear?

When you hear a message that says you, the child, are unacceptable, it's like seeing yourself in a cracked mirror. The reflection is distorted, and because you see that reflection, it changes your image of yourself. The cracked mirror reflects a child who is unworthy because of something that he or she has done. Of course, another reflection is also possible. When a child has done something wonderful in the eyes of his or her parents, the mirror shows someone who is attractive, appealing, and praiseworthy.

These images help make us who we are. As children, we

develop an internal dialogue with ourselves, with the self-voice saying things like "You have done well," "You need to do better," or "You have failed." That dialogue is formed by how we perceive we are responded to. We look in cracked mirrors and we get cracked reflections, giving us distorted images that we believe because they are the only representations of ourselves that we can see.

The Work of the Mirror

What were your mirrors? What have they told you about yourself and your own worthiness? It may surprise you how easy it is to find out. Even though the self-voice is a part of each person's internal makeup, you can become aware of it very quickly with some evaluative questions. Is the self-voice punitive? Is it demanding? Does it set goals so high that they are absolutely unreachable? If so, that droning, nagging, and incessant voice sets the stage for performance addiction.

It may be impossible to silence that voice because it is so much a part of your development. Yet I believe it is possible to separate it from who you are. You have to recognize where that voice comes from, what it's saying, and how it influences the mirrored image you have of yourself. The questions I posed at the beginning of this chapter will help you to evaluate your own level of understanding about your self-voice. Here they are again:

Can you engage in relaxing activities without thoughts that you are being lazy or slacking off?

Some people immediately answer, "Of course I can." And then they cite examples. They talk about going to the health club and working out. Or taking a weekend vacation at a B&B in the country. Or spending time in the sauna.

But if you have performance addiction, the time at a health club, which initially might be relaxing, soon turns into setting goals for losing weight, building lean body mass, or accomplishing an increasingly challenging set of repetitions.

How about that relaxing weekend vacation at the bed-and-breakfast? Did you take along a phone and keep it charged just in case? How many times did you think of the work you were neglecting or the tasks that you would face when you got home? And how much time did you spend thinking about the next week-end activity or event?

Much has been written about the burden of the 24/7 lifestyle. Phones follow us everywhere. We constantly check e-mails. Work pursues us from office, to home, to car, plane, and train. It's sometimes difficult to remember that none of this is being forced on us. We can turn off phones and computers. But many of us can't turn off the self-voice that says, "You're being irresponsible" or "You're missing an opportunity."

What are the thoughts and feelings that accompany your moments of relaxation? Do these moments require justification in your own mind? When you relax, do you know instinctively that you will have to pay for your downtime by working harder in the future? If you have performance addiction, the breaks are almost impossible to relish without hearing the self-voice that tells you to get moving again, to accomplish something, and to stop being lazy.

Is there a parent or spouse whom you feel you can never please for very long?

What could be more natural than a child who seeks parental approval? At first, it is a blind search that relies on a trial-and-error approach. A child tries out something new or something that gets noticed and is either punished or rewarded. A lesson is learned. Then the action is tested again, and if the message is consistent—if the child is repeatedly punished for some behaviors and rewarded for others—then he or she quickly develops a definition of what it means to satisfy his or her parent.

That's a comfortable feeling. The parent smiles, pats the child on the head, or gives the child a hug. All is well until the parent becomes withdrawn, angry, or indifferent. Then it is time once again to go searching for a rewarding sign of attention.

The meaning of love is so often defined by the way it is expressed within the family that we naturally search for partners who reward us in the same ways. If we used certain behaviors to elicit approval and attention from a parent, we will try similar behaviors to get the equivalent from a spouse. But how long does the reward last? When will it be withdrawn?

If you were appreciated only for how you performed, there is no such thing as a feeling of unconditional love. Approval and reward are so interconnected that they are inseparable in the child's mind . . . and in the adult's. Love feels conditional. To seek approval is to seek affection, and disapproval is synonymous with condemnation.

Not surprisingly, the spouse of someone who has performance addiction may feel an inordinate amount of power in the relationship. When two partners with performance addiction are involved in a relationship, the incessant need for approval on both sides translates into a constant struggle to communicate through the approval system rather than with forthright communication. When attention or praise is a constant prerequisite of affection, it's no wonder that some relationships swing up and down.

Almost inevitably, the child–parent relationship that has been built on performance expectations will evolve into a spousal relationship with a similar structure. We want our partners to approve of us the way our parents once did. If the self-voice is telling us what thoughts, behaviors, actions, and accomplishments are worthy of approval, then we are likely to become deaf to voices of unconditional love. How could it be possible for someone else to love us for who we are rather than for what we do?

Do you ever truly enjoy your work without being focused on the dollar amount of your efforts?

Take the example of Bret, a day trader. He made half a million dollars in a year and then lost almost all of it. A graduate of Yale, he comes from a conservative Texas family. Neither parent was very expressive, but Bret found he could talk to his father about money. In fact, that was the only thing that Bret and his father ever conversed about.

His dad was very proud of having started his own business. It had prospered, but the whole time Bret was growing up, his father worked overtime and never made it to any of Bret's athletic events, which were important to the young athlete. Thus, Bret's choice of career. In fact, he and his father actually traded together for three years, but their disagreements became more and more frequent and finally unbearable.

Bret decided to forgo having children. He didn't want anything interfering with his career and financial pursuits. Today he deeply regrets his choice, and his wife has never forgiven him. He has come to realize that he didn't want children because he was afraid to repeat his relationship with his father and relive all those painful experiences.

When Bret is losing, he tends to overreact and make reckless choices. He never tells his father about those days. But on a good day, it's different. "I call him after a big win," says Bret. "But I always feel disappointed. It's not that my dad doesn't respond, but it never seems related to me. It's as if he is focused exclusively on the money, the trade, quizzing me about the stock because he can't wait to get in on the action. All I want is for is for him to say I'm great. Instead, he is essentially saying, 'Show me how to make this money.' It seems so self-serving. All my life I have worked so very hard to be great to someone, and it never seems to quite happen."

Bret is an extreme example. Not everyone calls a parent when they make a killing in the stock market or even when they get a big raise. But the form of self-measurement is common. How much is your worth as a human being measured by your salary, your bank account, or the success of your investments?

For Bret, the stakes are very high. Money is more than income. It represents transcendent status or achievement. It is a means of communicating with his father. But in return for his reports of successful investments, he wants more than praise or congratulations. Bret is searching for the reassurance from his father that he is great.

Can you separate the effort and enjoyment of your work from the dollar rewards? Often, making lots of money and enjoying our work become so intertwined that it's impossible to distinguish one from the other. But it's worth asking whether the pursuit of money has become the most important factor when you make choices about your time, your work, and your lifestyle. For performance addicts, there can never be enough money, just as it is impossible for them to ever work hard enough or play well enough. Money is more than net worth. It becomes the measure of self-worth. If you need a dollar accumulation to demonstrate that you are outperforming yourself, work can never be satisfying enough. No amount of cash can ever say, "You're great!"

Do you strive to please authority figures such as bosses or managers without ever feeling secure about their approval?

When understanding, affection, and love are all conditional upon approval, you grow up in an atmosphere of uncertainty. The parental message "We will love you and stand by you no matter what you do" is transformed into "Be careful, do the right thing, check with us often, and we'll evaluate your performance." The latter communication, of course, is not that of parents who give unconditional love. It is the message of parents who need to control the thoughts, behavior, and emotions of their child.

It's not surprising that if you have performance addiction, you need regular communication from an authority figure. Note that this communication does not necessarily have to be either approval or disapproval. Even by withholding a clear message, the authority figure is highly influential. So you find yourself playing a guessing game to find out more than what the parent figure (manager, teacher, boss) is feeling as well as thinking. If you fall down in your performance, will this "parent" still like you and approve of you? Trying to determine this answer is so crucial that guessing can become an all-encompassing activity.

One of my clients, Diane, is a twenty-four-year-old graduate student working toward a Ph.D. in history. She has been successful throughout her academic career. Her father, a professor, was constantly urging her to excel. He pushed her to pursue graduate school. But in the summer after her first year of grad school, Diane's father was tragically killed in a car accident.

Midway through her second year, Diane has found that she can't complete a paper that should be well within her grasp. She realizes what has happened. What she wants from her professor is more than a grade, a comment, or help with the work. "I know I have this all out of perspective," she says, "but I want him to be very impressed. I want him to love me." Then she retracts. "I don't mean that—not like a love relationship."

But I think she does mean a love relationship. She knew that her father based all his responses on her performance. Many times, Diane acknowledged, "My father will never change." But that was when he was still alive—when the possibility of change still existed. Now the situation is quite different. Her father has disappeared from her life without leaving behind any final message to tell her whether she succeeded or failed in his eyes. There are no more chances for him to approve of her and love her unconditionally. But wouldn't it be wonderful if this professor loved her like her father never did? She has narrowed a lifetime of longings to one paper, one class, and one professor. If she pulls it off, this mirror of her self will show her someone who is appealing and approved of. If all goes well, she can reconstruct her childhood.

Do you long for a certain kind of affection you feel you seldom receive?

For anyone who has been repeatedly tested, the testing of others becomes a habit. But what does testing have to do with feelings of affection? Everything . . . and nothing, depending on whether you believe that emotions are measurable.

In fact, I hear about emotional accountability all the time. It is a recurrent theme among those who have performance addiction. There are conditional statements: "If he truly cared for me, he would not . . ." There are levels of measurement: "If she cares for me as much as she says she does, she would . . ." And there's outright testing in situations that seem as carefully prepared as a board exam: "I have asked him for . . . and decided if he doesn't do it, this will tell me once and for all whether he really loves me."

Underlying the conditions, the measurement, and the testing is the question that cannot be answered by any of these methods: "Does he or she feel real affection for me?" On the face of it, this question can be answered only in emotional terms. Affection is such a complex web of immeasurable factors. It can be communicated in a caring glance or with a vacation on the Riviera. It can be expressed in the form of passionate lovemaking or in a flash of anxiety about another person's welfare. It can be a single moment of forgiveness or a lifelong commitment. And, as we all know, nearly every expression of affection can be seen in at least two ways (Does he really care about me? Or is he really just out for himself?) If you try to apply tests and measurements to such complex imponderables, the very nature of affection becomes infinitely confusing.

And this is precisely the confusion that's faced by those with performance addiction. When we are so accustomed to being measured, what are the terms by which we measure others? What conclusions do we draw about those who express affection toward us?

Do you feel jealous when others accomplish great things?

When Andy Warhol made his famous pronouncement about fifteen minutes of fame, he failed to mention one thing: there aren't enough fifteen-minute time slots. For the vast majority of us, the portion of fame we get will be approximately, or exactly, zero.

Fifteen minutes seems short enough. How on earth can you tolerate zero fame if you have performance addiction? How do you know you've won unless the world acknowledges it? You need those headlines, if only for a moment.

Performance addicts have a great capacity to be distracted by the perceived greatness of others. I say *perceived* because it does not really matter whether the object of envy is actually more accomplished, skilled, or exceptional. The most distinguishing characteristic is fame itself. The qualities that helped facilitate notoriety (whether self-serving or not) are less significant than the simple fact that this envied person somehow made it.

If you are performance addicted, you're not just measuring yourself against those who get their names in the paper, their profiles in *Fortune,* or their photographs in *People.* Everyone is a yardstick. Comparisons are incessant. Even a neighbor can be intimidating.

I am reminded of Ralph, the manager at a prestigious Boston bank, who has been struggling to understand the roots of his performance addiction. The story he tells about his neighbor provides a clue. This isn't the usual case of keeping up with the Joneses. The neighbor's house is no bigger or more lavishly furnished than Ralph's. The neighbor does not drive a better car or hold a better job. Yet, for some reason, Ralph feels inferior.

When he discovers the root of his deferential behavior, it's an embarrassment. "My neighbor is a Yale graduate and I never graduated from college. I know I shouldn't feel inferior in his presence, but I do. It's insane. On an intellectual level I know I'm intelligent, but emotionally I never really outgrew my parents' negative perception of me. Growing up, I felt stupid. I heard over and over again how intelligent my sister was; she went to college and then graduate school. I can still hear those comparisons. They're as real to me now as if they had just been spoken yesterday."

Do you often pick out faults or imperfections in those who are close to you, even when you try to be more tolerant?

In one of their studies of perfectionism, Gordon Flett and Paul Hewitt found that this trait typically took three forms: self-oriented, other-oriented, and socially prescribed. It goes without saying that the person with performance addiction exhibits self-oriented perfectionism. You probably set unrealistic standards for yourself, then work relentlessly to fulfill those standards. But other-oriented perfectionism is another prominent characteristic of performance addiction. It is the equally unrealistic expectation that friends, families, or colleagues should meet certain fixed standards of behavior.

In fact, if you have performance addiction, you're constantly battling with other-oriented perfectionism. Not only do you make demands on yourself, but you also judge other people in similar ways. Why isn't your spouse more attentive? Why doesn't your friend dress better? Why don't your colleagues get things done faster?

Small complaints become persistent. Not only do you cease to forgive and forget, but you find yourself becoming less tolerant of people as intimates. Their failure to live up to expectations is an encroachment on your own self-image. If you have performance addiction, the imperfections of friends and family members can feel maddening. Impatience, intolerance, and even rage become directed toward those who just don't cut the mustard.

Is it difficult for you to stay focused when a spouse, child, or coworker is speaking?

In a survey of multitasking, researchers found that 54 percent of workers read e-mails while talking on the phone. Another 18 percent commonly review printed material when they're on the phone. And 14 percent say that they are capable of doing online shopping or research while holding a conversation.

The onslaught of multimedia communication has been accompanied by the inevitable proliferation of multitasking. "Connectedness has brought a glut," says Gleick. "We complain about our oversupply of information. . . . We treasure it nonetheless. We aren't shutting down our e-mail addresses. On the contrary, we're buying pocket computers and cellular modems and mobile phones with tiny message screens to make sure that we can log in from the beaches and mountaintops."

It might be argued that the need for staying in touch with others and keeping up the hectic pace is simply a basic requirement of daily living. Why forfeit these conveniences? For performance addicts, however, the tools of communication—the basic instruments of multitasking—are as necessary as addictive substances. Being disconnected or out of touch feels intolerable. If you're not distractedly busy, how important are you?

But if multichannel communication is essential for your feelings of self-worth, what happens if you slow down and just pay attention to one person at a time? What will you get out of the conversation? If you have performance addiction, the act of paying undivided attention to one other person seems dangerously like a waste of time. A conversation that is not action-focused, performance-oriented, or accomplishment-driven can make you feel extraordinarily restless.

If you find that you can't pay attention, even when you want to, your behavior is not necessarily a reflection of the esteem you have for a spouse, friend, or child but a more nagging sense of responsibility to your own self-voice. If that self-voice constantly asks, "What can this person help me accomplish?" "How can he or she perform better?" or "What is expected of me right now?" it stands to reason you cannot be present in the moment to just listen. Your multitasking is not just external. You must answer the e-mails of your self-voice that clamor for attention. You've got mail—and it comes from inside your head.

Do you often evaluate your appearance, intelligence, and material possessions?

Performance addiction can backfire in strange ways, especially when the self-voice cannot be silenced. "Are you thin enough?" the voice asks. "Are you smart enough?" "Do you have the lifestyle that you deserve?"

No external clues will answer these questions. Who, indeed, can tell you whether you are as beautiful, intelligent, or rich as you should be? A constant, reassuring, positive voice can be generated only from within yourself. But what if you never say to yourself, "You are as attractive as you can possibly be" or "You are making the most of your abilities"? Lacking the confidence and reassurance that such an inner voice would provide, you're sure to seek other forms of measurement.

When the only self-voice is highly critical, it can be very destructive. Case in point: Wendy has just returned from Palm Springs. How was her vacation? "Awful. I put on my two-piece—

the same one I wore last year—I looked disgusting. I've got a fat rear. I look ridiculous." But . . . how was the vacation? "I'm turning all wrinkly and blotchy. I'm turning into a dumpy old lady."

Where does the name-calling come from? Her distaste borders on revulsion. Is this really what Wendy thinks of herself? What is causing this self-punishment? Of course, her parents were the same way—always critiquing how she looked. But, she says, she doesn't want to blame her parents.

I suggest that she doesn't have to blame them. But there's something she does need to do if she's going to block the name-calling. She has to find out who the assailant is. What is this cruel voice that tells Wendy she's so disagreeable-looking that she literally disgusts herself? The scathing words come from the deep-rooted assumption that there must be something wrong with her. She compares herself to some standard that is set way too high and keeps telling herself, "I'm no good."

The unforgiving process of comparison is one of the classic expressions of performance addiction. It can apply to anything you do—words, actions, thoughts, appearance. No matter how good you are, someone is better. No matter how attractive you are, someone is vastly more handsome or beautiful. You can strive but never arrive. And when you fail yourself, your self-voice tells you that you are deplorable.

Everyone longs for an understanding self-voice. But performance addicts hear only the punitive one. The longing to be understood rather than measured becomes intense, taking you on a search for a more generous voice that will tell you the story of a worthier person.

The Forgiving Voice

The questions I ask in this chapter provide some ways to help you understand the fundamental characteristics of performance addiction. But just because you have some of these traits does not mean that you need to be a victim of this addiction. You can stop comparing yourself to others. You do not need to set the bar higher tomorrow than it was set today. You can enjoy the luxury and affluence that lie within reach without longing for more. You can relish the time shared with a spouse, child, colleague, parent, or sibling without worrying about your day's to-do list, your incoming e-mails, or your unanswered phone messages.

True, someone has to give you permission for all this to happen. Ideally, you could go back, fix the cracked mirrors, and admire your true reflection. You could elicit retractions from the people who continually told you to reach your potential, clean up your act, stop wasting time, or be all you can be. You could stand your ground against the parent who is disappointed in your attitude, the teacher who says you aren't showing much effort, the coach who wonders whether your heart is really in it, or the boss who declares you aren't meeting your goals.

Ideally, every article about a hopelessly rich family would tell you about their unhappiness and every photograph of a gorgeous person would be accompanied by a disclosure about the health costs of dieting. But as we all know, our families, schools, and society in general have numerous ways to reinforce performance addiction and few ways to alleviate it. The pressures for achievement are ever greater while the comforts are few. And, ultimately, the permission for relief can come from only one person. As you've probably guessed by now, that person is you.

Go back to the first question: *Can you engage in relaxing activities without thoughts that you are being lazy or slacking off?* Can you alter the tone of that harsh self-voice that accuses you of being lazy or slacking off? Can you read a book for pleasure, for instance, without reminding yourself that you have to finish the day's to-do list or accomplish what you promised you would do? If you know the origins of that voice, you can discover and learn ways to respond. You can find a tone that reflects more understanding and words that are more forgiving.

You no longer have to search for your reflection in cracked mirrors. You can replace them with a whole mirror that provides a true image. You can find a self-voice that is far more tolerant of who you really are—a voice that does not demand the impossible. There is no reason why performance addiction needs to control your attitude or your life.

As Victor Frankl said in *The Will to Meaning*, "Success and happiness must happen, and the less one cares for them, the more they come." I consider it my task to help you become less extreme about achievement, prosperity, good looks, fame, and wealth. I share Frankl's belief that the less you care for those things, the more they will come.

4

The Scene of
the Crime

1. When you have conflicts with people, do the things that bother you seem like old arguments that you've had before?

2. Do you react too strongly to the same type of person or the same situation over and over again?

3. How was praise expressed in your family? Was it more focused on achievement, on your character (personal traits such as honesty and integrity), or a balance of both?

4. When you're in a situation that calls for a change, do you find yourself trying to keep the situation static?

5. Do you often feel people don't really listen to you?

IN DESCARTES' ERROR, THE FIRST of Antonio Damasio's books about the relationship between functional brain neurology and the origin of the emotions, he uses the phrase "background feelings" to describe low-grade and sometimes intense emotions that catch us by surprise. Damasio's second book, *The Feeling of What Happens*, further develops this concept of background feelings and describes them in the following way: "Sometimes we become keenly aware of them and can attend to them specifically. Sometimes we do not and attend, instead, to other mental contents. In one way or another, however, background feelings help define our mental state and color our lives."

Damasio surmises that background feelings arise from what he distinguishes as "background emotions," which are communicated to other people in many ways. We give away our background emotions, he suggests, with body posture and with the tone and inflection of our voice. There is, therefore, a close relationship between background feelings and the drives of which we are more fully aware. Similarly, background feelings are also closely related to the moods we experience. "Moods," says Damasio, "are made up of modulated and sustained background feelings as well as modulated and sustained feelings of primary emotions."

What are the background feelings that influence your behavior? Can you tell when those feelings make you react or respond to people in certain ways? This is what I call your *hardwiring*.

Suppose I were to place you in a room by yourself, looking through a one-way mirror. On the other side of the mirror are ten people. You don't know any of them. You've never seen them before. Each one is distinctively dressed and looks quite different from the others. They are men and women of all ages. Obviously, they can't see you, so they can't relate to you in any way. And even though you can see them, you can't hear what they're saying.

Which person would you be most comfortable with? I am quite sure you can instantly choose someone. But suppose I ask you why. Can you give me a clear answer?

Let's run through the possibilities. Perhaps the person you selected has certain gestures that you find reassuring. Or maybe there are cosmetic aspects that win you over—let's say, what that person wears, the eye color, the hairstyle. But you didn't have to analyze all those factors in order to come up with your selection. You just *knew*. Right away, you had a feeling about the person you could be comfortable with.

That's your hardwiring. The person who makes you feel most comfortable initiates a background feeling that stirs certain moods and emotions that can be very roughly translated as "feeling right."

But here's the hitch: Sometimes our hardwiring leads us down the garden path. We make choices that may feel right based on our response to people but may be far from right in terms of where we are in our lives right now and what we need in our relationships. To restate the truism that those who do not recognize their errors are doomed to repeat them, I would say this: *If you do not recognize your hardwiring, you are fated to relive past relationships.*

Look at Your Hardwiring

Once you see how you're hardwired, I believe you'll have a much better understanding of how you respond to certain individuals. And once you see why and how you respond, I believe you'll have greater freedom, more options, and increased opportunities.

JODIE: HER PAST INTRUDES ON THE PRESENT

Jodie, a divorcée in her forties, has recently started dating again. She meets a man on a blind date who is immediately attractive to her. (This is her background feeling about the guy.) Handsome, well educated, and articulate, he talks about his previous marriage and about his young daughter, who is obviously very important to him. During the course of the evening, he says to Jodie, "I never thought I would meet a quality person like you."

Jodie feels herself being drawn in. Here is a man who idealizes her, which has always been important to her. Her response is hardwired. Jodie's father left her family when she was very young. She loved him, wanted him back, and felt that he had literally left her (rather than her mother or the family situation). As this new man in her life looks into her eyes and tells her she is a "quality person," Jodie has a powerful, positive response. She wants to be caught up and swept away, respected and adored at last. But Jodie has learned something about herself—that the hardwired emotional response, however instinctively right it may seem, is just one of many possible responses to this man.

"This guy has no idea who I am," Jodie reminds herself. "I could be a nightmare, for all he knows." Instead of being caught up in the wonderful experience of being idealized, as she had been in the past, Jodie has a real sense of what's going on inside her—that is, what background feelings are dictating her response. "Because of my father leaving us when I was young, I have always longed for an older man's attention," she says. "As soon as I get that idealizing look, I fall, especially for a man who needs to be mothered."

Jodie knows her vulnerabilities today, so she can prevent herself from responding to the situation in a very biased way. But how would that be possible unless she could recognize her own hardwiring?

The fact is, you can't see yourself and others clearly unless you factor in the old hurts that cloud your judgment. One scene from the past can be repeated through all of life's sequences. In Jodie's case, her father's leaving her (and her family) was a scene that would be repeated in some way every time a man was attracted to her. In the replay she would always hope for the outcome that was never possible with her father—to be idealized, comforted, and cared for. That was in her hardwiring. But now she can identify how her judgment is clouded by background feelings and realize that this relationship is not an avenue toward rebuilding her past. She will have to mend her fences in other ways.

Where Is Your Scene of the Crime?

For Jodie, it was never easy to return to the scene of the crime. She had to go back to the year, the day, the very hour when her father deserted the family and essentially abandoned his young daughter. She had to recall what that felt like, then think about the ramifications of that moment.

What does a young girl experience when her father disappears? What is he saying to her with his absence? What does she need from him that she will never get, and how does that affect her view of other men as father figures, lovers, or potential husbands?

These scenes are so painful! I want to make it clear that I am not recommending that you go through an unnecessary examination of the past. Such a close look, in my view, is worthwhile only as a way for you to understand how your past interferes with your present behavior. Otherwise, there's a risk that you're dwelling on the past as a way to avoid moving forward. I'd like you to be able to (as one of my clients put it) look at the past but not stare.

Can you see what got you hardwired in the first place? With that insight you'll have more freedom because you'll know where the background feelings are coming from, and your present-day emotional responses won't seem so controlling. This is what I mean by mending fences. Obviously, you can't go back in time and try to alter the personalities of your parents or change your relationships with other authority figures.

I have certainly met people who would just like to get revenge (as if that were possible) after discovering the scene of the crime. I know others who would only like to grieve, as if touching deep despair could fix what went wrong. And still others who go for mockery, deriding parents or authority figures who scarred them. But none of these attitudes is actually very helpful if you're going to mend your own hurt. Rage, grief, and mockery are acute and understandable reactions. As we all know, however, they cannot repair the past or provide adequate compensation.

But what if you can recognize what happened? Then you have some perspective. You can understand your background feelings and the moods they engender. Building upon that kind of understanding, you have the opportunity to open new avenues for yourself.

Right now, you can take a short quiz that will help you

uncover the scene of the crime in your own history. This is a necessary starting point as you begin to explore the performance addiction issues addressed in subsequent chapters. Be honest as you answer the questions in the following self-evaluation. Write down the answers and use them as a starting point for further reflection.

Self-Evaluation:
Searching for Your Scene of the Crime

1. Is it typical of you to react intensely to day-to-day situations? (Examples: Your spouse burns the toast and you're furious. Your spouse is twelve minutes late for dinner and you give him or her the silent treatment. Your roommate forgot to take out the trash and you're exasperated.)

2. Do you realize that your level of intensity is often an indicator of past unresolved conflicts—essentially a cue that you're returning to the scene of the crime? (If you overreact when your spouse leaves a dish in the sink overnight, consider whether this is the same reaction you got from your mother or father for the same behavior.)

3. Are you aware of how the deepest hurt you have experienced in your life still influences your current behavior? Do you factor in your bias so that you don't overreact? (Example: Suppose your mother used to criticize you frequently for not excelling academically. Do you have great difficulty today accepting constructive criticism from a supervisor, teacher, or adviser? Are you aware of how your past sensitivity influences your current reality?)

4. Have you spent time trying to understand how your past influences your current life, or do you tend to think the past has little bearing on your current behavior?

5. Do you consider yourself to be quite sensitive to how you're perceived?

6. Are you sensitive about your accomplishments? Your financial status? Your appearance? Your level of education?

7. What experiences in the past created these sensitivities?

8. How do they interfere with how you perceive yourself and others today?

9. Think of a key person in your past and imagine that person holding a mirror in front of you so that you can see your own level of capability. Do you still see yourself as the person reflected in that mirror?

10. Think about the people who "held up the mirrors" in your past. In your recollection, were they capable of giving you a true picture of yourself?

11. Do you realize that people and situations that feel right immediately may be deceiving? Familiarity can breed instant comfort and eventual distress.

12. Have you identified how your past has created certain vulnerabilities for you?

13. Do those close to you currently know how your hard-wiring influences you today?

14. Can you explain in detail how your scene-of-the-crime experiences influence your current reality?

15. Do you have friends or family who can help you understand how powerful experiences in your past distort your view of yourself and others?

As you reflect on your answers to these questions, what are the moments that you most vividly recall? Perhaps there was a time in your life when a parent deserted you, a promise was not kept, or a confidence was betrayed. Or there may have been an extended time in your childhood when your self-image was eroded by constant criticism or caustic remarks. Back at the scene of the crime, perhaps you became invested with your parents' delusions of grandeur. Or you grew up with the notion that your performance could compensate for the breakdown of a family or conflicts between your parents. How you find these scenes, how you deal with their emotional content, and how you use this knowledge today to make better decisions about your life are critical factors in confronting your performance addiction.

Do You Feel That Your Views Are Acceptable?

"Am I being taken seriously?" I suppose every one of us has asked ourselves that question. Most of the time we can say, "I hope so." But what if you aren't taken seriously? What if your thoughts are derided, you're told to be ashamed of your feelings, or your opinions are met with rage? That's a violation of trust.

Jean: Humiliated by the Principal

In one of our group meetings, Jean tells us about her hallway encounter with her principal. Jean is the chairwoman of the English department in her high school, the youngest person ever to hold this position. She wrote an innovative proposal for next year's curriculum—a plan that won approbation from other teachers in her department. The principal saw the proposal and was extremely critical. But instead of meeting with Jean and discussing it with her, the principal took advantage of a chance hallway encounter to lash into her, objecting to the suggested changes in the curriculum.

As Jean tells the group about this experience, she is irate. It was the end of the day and other teachers were walking by. Any number of them overheard the principal berating her.

Do we know why Jean is outraged? It's a public humiliation. Her carefully developed and sincerely expressed ideas have been held up for public derision. And yet the scenario is a little more complicated than that. In the past, Jean has portrayed this authority figure as "a troubled woman . . . very controlling, always critical of something." She is not alone in her assessment. Jean says that many of her fellow teachers share her view. And the superintendent, who is a longtime friend of Jean's, has confided that she, too, is aware of the principal's history of erratic behavior.

As Jean talks about this incident, other group members respond to her outrage with intense expressions of their own anger. What was the principal's assumed right to confront Jean in public? Jean's proposal had been carefully thought out and well considered. Yet her principal was treating it quite irrationally as though it were some kind of personal affront to her authority. "I was so embarrassed," says Jean. "But there she was *yelling* at me in the hall in a completely unprofessional way as other teachers walked by."

Where did the embarrassment originate? Clearly, the principal had acted inappropriately. So it was she who should have been embarrassed, not Jean. But the critical question is: *If someone is yelling at you in the hallway and you are not speaking, what is your crime?*

It was actually someone else in the group who gave us some insight. "It would be ideal if I could see that when someone else is acting impulsively, I should not be the one embarrassed. What am I guilty for? But it's not so easy to see if you came from a family with an extremely critical parent like my father. I always thought that when he went off on me, it was my fault."

When this has been your experience of a parent or authority figure—that is, someone who criticizes you harshly for expressing your views—the scene of the crime makes you extraordinarily vulnerable. Your trust has been broken! Just consider how that happened to Jean. At the request of the principal, Jean gave her honest opinion. She left herself open. Having invested in a proposal that she truly believed in, she was vulnerable. And what was her reward? The principal degraded her. She felt unjustly and publicly berated, chided, and humiliated.

But what really happened? The principal had behaved inappropriately. From the viewpoints of all the teachers who overheard this interchange, it was not Jean who had humiliated herself but the principal. Even the superintendent recognized that the principal had personal issues that interfered with her effectiveness as an administrator. This is the power of hardwiring—to convince you that you're guilty or unworthy even when you're not.

When you have been told that your views, beliefs, or emotions are unacceptable, it may take a long time before you realize that you don't have to be ashamed or embarrassed when you declare how you feel or explain what you believe in. When you are confronted by authority figures who say, "Your views are unacceptable," you need to be prepared to reject humiliation and embarrassment. Believe me, these are *imposed* emotions. The crime is not yours. The authority figure who speaks to you now is not the same person who blamed you in the past. You can choose to respond differently, and when you do, you free yourself from the hardwired response that originated at the scene of the crime.

Have a Good Look at Your Good Self

The following story about Laura, a client of mine, is a poignant example of how a well-intentioned parent set the stage for her daughter to have a lifelong battle with body image. Clearly, Laura's mother wanted to save her daughter from the torment that she herself had experienced. But unwittingly, the mother laid the foundation for the same struggle to be re-created.

Laura: Always Feeling Fat

Laura's mother was obese. When Laura was growing up, she also had a weight problem. By the time Laura reached adolescence, she was a lightning rod for her mother's disapproval. If she didn't lose weight, her mother reminded her, she would be depriving herself of all kinds of opportunities.

Fat girls don't attract good-looking boys, her mother told her. Even worse, if she was overweight, people would think she was sloppy and lazy. They would think she didn't take care of herself.

So when Laura and her mother argued about food, it was never just about food. The fight escalated. Didn't Laura have any self-discipline? Why did she have to take another piece of bread? Was she really hungry or eating just to get on her mother's nerves?

There were lectures and tears. When spats erupted at mealtimes, Laura's father left the table. Silences, not-so-subtle suggestions, and even glances became fuel for the fires of adolescent outrage: Why do you keep watching me? You're keeping me prisoner. I hate you. Why do you care what I eat? Ultimately, Laura confronted her mother: "You think I'm going to be fat because *you're* so fat."

After the storming about, the tears, and the rage, there would be prolonged silences. But if Laura wore clothing that looked too tight, or got caught grabbing an extra cookie, it started all over again. The adolescent rage was real, and it was strong. But rage alone could not repair Laura's abused self-image. Now, as a thirty-seven-year-old adult, Laura makes fun of her "big butt," her "thunder thighs," and her "pudge."

In many other respects, Laura feels a reasonable amount of confidence and self-esteem. She is a professional woman with a high income. She's proud of what she has accomplished. Yet she is still searching for some approval that will make it okay for her to be comfortable with the body she has been given.

The approval is not there, of course, so instead she has gone searching for the perfect guy. She wants someone gorgeous. According to her hardwiring, if she finds him, everything will be all right.

No parent will ever be arrested for telling a child that she needs to lose weight or blaming her for being too fat. But a child's self-esteem does get abused in this type of situation. Today, it is impossible for Laura to look at herself in the mirror without embarking on meticulous self-measurement.

Instinctively, her visual calipers go to work, performing a daily ritual as she measures her appearance against some higher standard of slimness and beauty. What eludes her is an impossible physical perfection—the Laura who could be, the Laura who might be. And under the terms of this measurement, the Laura she sees in the mirror always falls short of the ideal.

Of course, I don't have to remind you of the occasional horrors and multiple dangers of adolescence. We all survived those years when egos are exquisitely fragile and self-assertion turns to querulous outrage. It is almost too easy for someone's offhand remark, especially a parent's, to become a locus of pain.

As adolescence passes, the strong emotional reactions subside to a dull roar. But during that time, you actually go through a neurological change that affects how you behave in the future. Were you ever called stupid, lazy, fat, or queer? Yes, it's possible you developed a thick skin. But some of those messages got encoded in your mind. If the negative slur matched a negative image that was created in your family, then it probably stuck.

Right now, you may be attempting to erase that image and create a new one. It's hard work. But you've got a big investment. You have to make sure no one will ever see you in that hurtful way again.

TERENCE: IN SEARCH OF THE PERFECT PERFORMANCE

One of my clients, Terence, is a very fine musician. His father, however, did not exactly encourage him. "Musicians are a dime a dozen," his father told him. "You'll never make anything of yourself unless you're one of the greatest."

Terence recalls a school dramatic production in which he

had to play the piano. He struck a few wrong chords and the kids in the auditorium erupted with hoots and hollers. His goal today is to be the best in the business so that he can never be criticized by anyone again.

Of course, Terence will be criticized. So will you. The real issue is what you will hear when criticism is offered. Will you only hear a parent's exasperated voice saying something like "You'll never make anything of yourself"? Will you hear the catcalls of fellow students? "That is all so far in the past," you may be saying to yourself. But those old hurts can spawn a lifelong attempt to perfect a certain fantasized image that will supposedly protect you. If you were mauled once, you'll work very hard to make sure it doesn't happen again.

Where are the mirrors that reflect who you are today? How can you get feedback that is not distorted by the echoes of old, familiar, critical voices?

There is a way out, but to find it you have to find truthful mirrors. You need to objectively hear the feedback you receive today without reliving past encounters. Once you can recognize the old hurts, you'll have an opportunity to begin truly fresh relationships without trying to revise and remake the past.

Were You Born a Hotshot?

In many instances the drive to excel, the obsession to be extraordinary, creates what we least expect. Instead of gaining a position of "specialness" in relation to others, we drive away those who are closest to us. Roy's perspective on life tells us to pay close attention to the effects of needing to be number one.

ROY: THE SPORTS CAR IMAGE

"I'm like a Ferrari," says Roy. "I'm just a high-maintenance kind of guy." As arrogant as this sounds, Roy has such a winning way of expressing himself that the group listening to him is more amused than offended. And his remark needs to be put in context. He is in group therapy. And he has just described how difficult it is for his wife to put up with him. After all, how many women dream of sharing an emotional life with a high-maintenance Ferrari?

His description seems justified. Roy *is* high maintenance. He demands a lot and has achieved a great deal. Roy is a top executive for a global clothing manufacturer. His annual six-figure salary is only part of a compensation package that runs in the millions. His good mind, excellent education, and gold-plated MBA helped get him where he is today. His drive, charm, and self-confidence are all evident.

Because Roy and I have talked about his family, especially his father, it seems clear where the Ferrari image comes from. His father is a motivational speaker but not just any motivational speaker. "I am one of the four or five most sought after speakers in the country" is the way he described himself to Roy. Although Roy respects his father and his opinions, the self-aggrandizement in that statement is so obvious that even Roy is not deluded. But even more significant is the fact that Roy's father, who easily recalls the names of scores of valuable clients, can't remember the name of Roy's wife. He keeps calling her Karen, but her name is Kara. So the man who bills himself as a top-ranked professional in dealing with human relationships cannot even grasp the name of his own daughter-in-law.

There is a disconnect, and it has been passed on from father to son. The son needs a glorified self-image that is simply a delusion of grandeur—that he is a Ferrari. Not a Ford. Not a Chevy. His self-image is the desirable, perfect, expensive vehicle he has always wanted to own.

But the Ferrari has a problem. Far from paying a lot of attention to her high-maintenance guy, Kara has developed an interest in another man—a divorcé who was recently hired by her accounting firm. Roy is deeply unhappy. The trouble is, he can't reconcile his personal unhappiness with the image of himself as a sleek, well-maintained, expensive vehicle.

The Ferrari image is built upon a status symbol, not a sense of self. But there is a price to be paid for such a self-concept. It is what Tim Kasser calls "contingent self-esteem" in *The High Price of Materialism*. It is contingent upon meeting particular external standards.

"When such individuals are successful at meeting their goals," says Kasser, "they experience positive feelings. Such positive feelings tend to be short-lived, however, and the sense of worth is fairly unstable, as new challenges and threats quickly arise that can easily deflate their self-esteem."

For Roy, the deflation of his self-image was so catastrophic that it challenged his most fundamental view of himself. *He* was the Ferrari—not the divorced guy in his wife's accounting firm. *He* was the one who needed to be treated like a high-maintenance vehicle. Didn't his wife realize that? Her attention was slipping away along with the vestiges of Roy's self-esteem.

Roy feels as if his wife owes him loyalty, respect, love, and honor for the wonderful performance that he has turned in. Her wavering attention is intense punishment. But if he wants to find her again, he will have to give up his Ferrari image and become more human. The question is: Can he discover a less-than-perfect self whom he can also accept?

Did Your Parents Invest in You?

To some parents, children are clearly an investment in the future. The investment can take many forms. Perhaps the parents think it is the child's responsibility to follow in their footsteps—to achieve the financial means required to look after the welfare of the entire family or to take care of them in their old age. Other children are invested with expectations that go beyond security and accomplishment: they feel obligated to accumulate wealth or attain levels of social prestige that their parents are clearly unable to reach in their own lifetime.

In some families, such expectations are implicit rather than explicit. The child gets signals that he or she must constantly interpret. The child who continues to work hard and achieve new levels of competence is rewarded with parental endearments. But if that child goes his own way and stops responding to the signals that keep him on track, affection is abruptly withdrawn. Under these circumstances, children are predictably more likely to choose the behavior that earns them rewards rather than punishment. The child who succeeds provides her parents with the compensation they desperately need. The child who strays from the chosen path becomes, in a sense, an emotional outcast.

LEA: A HOSTAGE TO LOVE

Lea is an example of how parental controls become deeply embedded in a child's psyche. In her household, every day was dictated by family routine. Hours were allocated for tasks such as studying, chores, and family time. Apart from the family's immediate expectations concerning Lea's obligations, she was also reminded of communal responsibilities. "I felt like a hostage to love," says Lea. "They had so many rules and regulations, so many ways I could embarrass them among their friends."

At one point in high school, Lea strayed from the path by dating a black boy who came from Brazil. Every night, her father gave her lectures about Brazilian men and black men who were "going nowhere." Lea's father made it clear that he had utter disdain for such people. In Lea's family, the rules and regulations had one purpose: to ensure that the family's future was "going somewhere." Lea was born to be part of that. Her father warned that she was not going to throw herself away on some young man who would live out his life "in a one-room tenement in Boston." Lea would flee to her room and cry. Even there, she could not get away. At the sound of her sobs, her father or mother would come into her room and the lecture would begin all over again.

For performance addicts like Lea, the only way to obtain love is to be a hostage to someone else's demands. Of course, now that childhood is behind her, Lea can no longer trace the pattern of her success with an internal playbook describing the rules. Her relationships and her achievements now feel like they fall short because she gives up too much for too little in return. The more she exerts herself, the greater the compensation she feels she owes to her parents—for all they have done for her and for those few times when she broke the rules and strayed outside the boundaries. She is hardwired to be self-sacrificing, denying her own inclinations. She has learned that unless she is especially tuned to her parents' need for confirmation, she will experience the withdrawal of their affection.

What Were You Supposed to Be?

We are all familiar with the star teacher whose self-importance becomes entwined with the luminous talent or intelligence of a particular student. In a best-case scenario, the rewards go both ways. Young people can easily benefit from the knowledge and guidance of a dedicated teacher, who in turn is invigorated by the challenges inherent in mentoring an apt protégé. It is only when such a teacher relies on the star-pupil qualities of his or her student for affirmations of the teacher's own self-worth that the relationship becomes questionable. Who is most in need of the affirmations of success—the teacher or the pupil?

I see a similar paradigm in some families where a parent begins using a child for self-aggrandizement. The child learns that he or she needs to stay especially attuned to the parent's need for confirmation. And the threat for the child? If he withdraws his attention, there will be a commensurate withdrawal of love.

JOHN: THE DOCTOR WHO CAN'T HEAL HIS PAST

One of my clients, John, is a pediatrician. His father is a college president with a well-established academic reputation, but he has a fragile self-image. Throughout John's childhood, his father was constantly impressing him with his vast knowledge of an array of topics, from molecular biology and macroeconomics to car mechanics and personal finance. John learned to listen with rapt attention. "That's amazing," "That's incredible," and "How do you know all that?" became rote responses to his father's imparted wisdom. The payoff, of course, was enormous. His father spent many hours with John, sealing the closeness of their relationship and rewarding the boy's attentiveness with paternal love.

But there was a downside to this one-way communication that became apparent only when John began making decisions for himself. John's father expected him to listen. When John began to go his own way, his actions meant something far more threatening to his father than normal adolescent rebellion. To his father his actions represented rejection of his vast accumulation of knowledge. Approval was withdrawn and so was affection. John's father was deeply offended if his son made any decision without prior consultation.

Nor was it just his father who needed the support. John's parents were divorced when the boy was ten years old, and John's mother was devastated. She found herself alone in a midwestern town where her husband had taken a position at a liberal arts college just a year and a half before. John, her only child, became the person she turned to. She needed him to affirm her attractiveness and pump up her fragile ego.

Today, John is separated from his wife and daughter. The marriage lasted five years. His wife, like his mother, suffered from depression and insomnia, and she needed her fragile self-image to be constantly reaffirmed. John is hardwired to be self-sacrificing and supportive of others. He is a master at denying his own inclinations and presenting others with an incredibly flattering image of themselves. Often, if I render an insight, he will compliment me as if I have said something truly profound. He does not feel safe unless he is appeasing the ego of another person.

Changing Your Hardwiring

Performance addicts are likely to replay interactions that occurred at the scene of the crime. Even when we recognize what occurred—the exact circumstances that made us feel humiliated—we often go about rearranging ourselves so that the scene will never be repeated again. If someone criticized a body part in front of others, we try endlessly to change that physical aspect, or we go on hating ourselves for having the defect to begin with. The experience of feeling bad or feeling good may be so embedded in those past scenes that we can't be sure what feels good or bad right now. We can't access the old situation, speak to the sender of the message (parent, coach, or friend), and find out what message was truly meant. We can, however, truly understand the situation and the person who embarrassed, humiliated, or hurt us.

KURT: TAKING OLD BATTLES TO WORK

Kurt is project director at a large marketing firm, and a new vice president has just been brought in over his head to manage his division. Obviously, this situation could generate all kinds of workplace issues. Perhaps Kurt should resent the fact that someone outside the company has been brought in over him. Or he might resent being given new directives on projects that are already under way.

But when he tells the group about his recent experiences, we realize he's dealing with issues that go far beyond the workplace. "I'm staying late and I'm working my ass off," he says. "But the guy [the new vice president] says nothing. I mean, he's not complaining, but he is so emotionless. He doesn't give compliments. I keep trying and trying to get him to validate my performance."

Throughout the summer, Kurt worked many long days, overseeing the launch of a new product. This effort didn't seem to make any impression on his boss. "All he said was thanks. I mentioned it to him the other day, and he reminded me that we need to move forward."

Kurt finds it difficult to keep up the momentum when he's so alert to signals from his boss. "I can sense his disapproving eyes on me all the time. I don't know whether I'm paranoid or he is really so critical. I've got all my guys working extra hours—and no mention from him how we're doing. I don't think I can keep their spirits up as well as my own with this guy."

As people in the group listen to Kurt, they relate his experience to many of the issues that they, too, face at work: the controlling manager who seems indifferent to human interactions; the pressure to outperform, followed by disappointment that their efforts aren't rewarded; the need to get the approval of someone who seems intent on finding fault all the time.

But as we turn back to Kurt's specific situation, the discussion is redirected from workplace dynamics and issues of leadership and management to a topic that is far more intimate, personal, and hurtful. He has described his mother as a highly critical woman who never approved of her son. Throughout his childhood, he developed an attitude of perfectionism that essentially reinforced her message. And a pattern was established. He looked for ever-greater challenges, so he was constantly in over his head. But once he met each challenge and succeeded, the feeling of victory was short-lived, and he would have to start all over again.

Acceptance and approval were never there. No matter what he did, his mother would always disapprove. So it's not surprising that in the absence of any real empathy from his manager, Kurt assumes that he's not measuring up and not appreciated.

It makes perfect sense that he persists in trying to win over this boss because it simulates his experience with his distant, critical mother. I point out to Kurt that this pattern is really part of his hardwiring. As so often happens, we pick people who replicate the past.

"That makes so much sense," Kurt agrees. "I always dismiss people who are complimentary. And I seek out the people who are hardest to please."

As Kurt knows, it's very unlikely that a boss or manager will change very much. But the hardwiring *can* change. Kurt wonders aloud whether he has the energy and drive to make such a change.

As I point out, what are the alternatives? It takes a great deal of energy to maintain myths about ourselves. If Kurt believes he can't do anything right while the vice president thinks he's doing fine work, Kurt has to constantly rearrange the facts to fit his image of himself. He has to find out where he's failing and work to clean up the mess, which takes huge amounts of concentrated application and generates the most intense kind of stress. And for what? To reinforce the belief that he deserves the disapprobation that he feels.

What if that energy were redirected to changing his beliefs about himself? Kurt can't change his boss any more than he can change his height or the color of his eyes. But the truth about human nature is that anything that has been learned can be unlearned. Kurt is capable of unlearning that he's not good enough, that he messes things up, and that he deserves disapproval. He can actually change the hardwired myths. It's far more constructive for him to direct his efforts that way rather than use up all his energy trying to maintain the status quo.

Changing the Myth

If you've done the self-evaluation on pages 58–59, you've already taken an important first step toward discovering the scene of the crime in your personal history. After you've recognized those hardwired myths, the next step will be the important task of changing them so that patterns don't repeat themselves. This will take some unlearning, which can be difficult. It all begins with recognition. You have to access the scene-of-the-crime situation before you can begin dealing with the consequences of the myths that were established.

When I was eight years old, I was the youngest member of my Little League team. The coach had trouble with my name, so he decided to be flip about it.

"Okay, Semicola, Coca-Cola, or Pepsi-Cola . . . get up to bat!"

I froze. To this day, I still remember the name of that coach and the expression on his face when he humiliated me. But today, I realize he had little idea of how fragile a young person's self-worth is. He opted to satisfy his own need to be funny, with little understanding of the psyche of an eight-year-old.

The most revealing moments may be those that are most difficult to look at. If you are intensely embarrassed by someone's criticism, for instance, even though you know intellectually that the other person is being completely unreasonable, where does your discomfort originate? Can you identify the origins of your reaction? Are you reliving some experience rather than living this one? You're hardwired to feel responsible, to feel guilty for crimes you believe you committed in the past. But if you can identify the source of these feelings, you can reaccess them with today's more accurate vision.

What You Can Do about Performance Addiction

At the beginning of this chapter, I posed a number of questions about the scene of the crime. In the section below, you'll find some insights that will help you further understand each of those scene-of-the-crime issues.

When you have conflicts with people, do the things that bother you seem like old arguments that you've had before?

INSIGHT: The next time you feel pressure to perform at an exceptional level, try to identify whether the voice tells you to be someone different or someone better than who you are. Is it your mother's voice? Your father's? Where is the judgment coming from?

Now imagine that the judgmental voice is directed at someone else—not you. Try to describe what you hear. Are the words kind, loving, and generous? Or do you hear someone who is angry, demanding, and impatient? If you can describe the voice, you will get a vivid picture of that person as someone separate from you. What that person needed is not what you need for yourself.

Do you react too strongly to the same type of person or the same situation over and over again?

INSIGHT: Describe for yourself or someone else the exact character and motives of the person to whom you are reacting. If you are overreacting to a boss's criticism, for instance, it is probably because that person reminds you of a parent or another authority figure who hurt you in the past. But there are real differences between the person in the current scene and the authority figure in the original scene of the crime. To the extent that you can understand those differences and see them clearly, you will be able to respond appropriately rather than reacting with oversensitivity to some past hurt.

How was praise expressed in your family? Was it more focused on achievement, on your character (personal traits such as honesty and integrity), or a balance of both?

INSIGHT: If approval was mostly based on your performance rather than recognition of the essence of your character, you probably grew up thinking your value was exclusively determined by your status, possessions, and external success. It has been proven by many studies that this kind of external focus leads to much dissatisfaction. Often people work all their lives to achieve more and gain more possessions only to feel devastated when they discover that status and material gain do not in and of themselves lead to happiness and contentment.

Retrace how you came to be valued. Try to reexamine from a position of truth what really matters in terms of gaining love and approval. What has actually worked?

When you're in a situation that calls for change, do you find yourself trying to keep the situation static?

INSIGHT: If you grew up in an expectation-laden family, you may fear change. Because self-esteem and desirability are based on performance in this type of family, when you meet the criteria for temporary approval, you have to ask yourself what is next. You are thrown into anxiety when the criteria for success change. If your parents gave you affection based on how you performed, then you still need approval, because love is not a given. Love depends on external accomplishments. With change comes a new set of demands, and you have to worry about performance all over again.

The challenge now is to see yourself as acceptable, no matter what you achieve or how you perform. Imagine yourself being raised in an environment where your essence is seen as lovable.

People raised in a genuinely supportive environment are more resilient in the face of change. They don't fret when the conditions of their environments are altered, because they have the internal sustenance to weather the storm. They have faith that no matter what happens, they will be okay. When they behaved imperfectly in childhood, they were not rejected. Their parents might have been disappointed in a particular situation, but these children still felt loved despite the outcome of their performance.

Do you often feel that people don't really listen to you?

INSIGHT: If you were raised in a household that fostered performance addiction, it would not be surprising if you felt as if you were not heard. In such a family, a parent's needs come first; the child's feelings or wishes are rarely taken into account. You may have been told what to think, how to feel, and what you should aspire to. As a result, you may have an exquisite sensitivity about the way people listen and respond to you. In an environment that fosters performance addiction, others half listen, then drive the conversation in some direction more to their own liking.

People who are struggling with this aspect of performance addiction might be irritated with other people who interrupt them—say, at a party. If you find yourself reacting in this way, remind yourself that parties are not meant for one-on-one, in-depth conversations. Often, party conversation is just fast-paced banter. It's just a light means of connecting. Even good listeners will give themselves permission to interrupt and be playful, not intending to be offensive at all.

None of us can make up for what we were not given. That being said, however, you certainly have the right to be heard. But be careful that you don't overreact. In some gatherings, there is no demand for very attentive listening. Try to consider the norms for each particular situation.

5

Image Love and Your Relationships

1. Do you find yourself obsessed with a particular trait or physical aspect of another person?

2. Do you feel it is difficult to tolerate physical changes in your spouse or partner as time goes on?

3. Are you more comfortable with your spouse or lover when you are alone than when you're in public?

NONE OF US FALLS IN LOVE with another person. We fall in love with an image. In the obsession and compulsion of romantic passion, this image has the vividness of a magnificent photograph, the intensity of a romantic film score, and the sensual and intoxicating effects of a magic potion. We escape from time. We escape from responsibilities. For a while, a person in love is in a state of almost complete self-delusion. This is what I call *image love*.

Insofar as romantic love is seen as a form of intoxication and madness, I suppose I am simply in agreement with a long line of poets, novelists, filmmakers, and artists who have done their best to convey what it's all about. We'll never fully understand the measure of our need to be attached to another human in the most profound and meaningful ways.

But in some respects, image love is easy to explain. It is the all-encompassing experience that two people share before they get around to knowing each other. Many aspects of romantic love, which at first blush seem nuanced and deeply mysterious, become more understandable as two people embark on the longer process of self-exposure that occurs during years of cohabitation or matrimony. Sometimes, it is only when two people are deeply unhappy with each other and with their relationship that they can understand the illusions that veiled the details of their first contact with each other. Only with time and increased vulnerability can their relationship can be more fully understood—which brings us to Karen and Bob.

Karen and Bob: What They Saw (and Didn't See) in Each Other

They met at the University of Massachusetts. He was the lanky, blond-haired, blue-eyed pitcher on the baseball team. But Bob's athletic credentials, while impressive, were not what drew Karen to him. What she loved was his uninhibited style—the way Bob seemed to be totally oblivious to what anyone else thought. He wasn't rude or blustery. He just acted as if he had a commanding sense of himself.

Bob always seemed to know who he was, and that quality held enormous appeal for Karen. On the field and off, he was poised, skilled, and capable. When they went places together, he made friends quickly and easily. Karen, who had always felt like a pale presence at the edge of a crowd, never knowing exactly who she was or what she was doing, discovered that it was possible and even natural to be easy with people, oblivious to their expectations, and comfortable with companionship. The little voice in her head that kept judging her, making demands, and insisting on proprieties would switch off when she and Bob hung out together.

She felt, quite literally, like a new woman.

And a well-appreciated young woman, at that. Bob thought she was beautiful and said so. He loved being with her and said so. He didn't have to mull over his real feelings. He was self-confident and self-assured. From Bob's point of view, so long as he loved Karen, he would be equally loved in return.

His sense of confidence seemed justified. The year they graduated, the U-Mass baseball team made it to the Eastern finals. Bob did not delude himself with dreams of making the major leagues, but once he had his degree he figured his career path would be well paved. Sales or marketing were his most obvious choices. But whatever Bob did, he expected to rise fast.

Karen's was a more plodding course of achievement, and she felt as if she had to struggle hard for everything she got. But she assumed this was a part of her nature, and it paid off. She made the dean's list and got into Boston College's MBA program.

After Karen and Bob got married, Karen made her way through business school. A year after she finished, their son Patrick was born. Now Patrick is six, his younger sister Marjorie is four, and it's been four years since Bob last held a job. Karen comes alone to therapy. Bob is in rehabilitation in a hospital in Rhode Island, trying to cope with alcohol and gambling addictions. Karen takes care of the children, works full time, and takes the kids to see Bob on the weekends.

Karen wonders what happened to the man she fell in love with and married. The absent, unemployed father struggling with alcohol and gambling addiction miles away—geographically and mentally—from the woman he adored bears little resemblance to the eager, confident college student who was the epitome of grace, self-assurance, and conviviality.

Have time and events wrought a complete change? Or is this exactly the same Bob that she is now seeing clearly for the first time?

These aren't questions I have to ask Karen. Almost constantly, she is asking them herself. But there was no chance she could see him clearly back then.

Karen's father is a real estate attorney. Karen's mother, a beautiful woman who was pampered and admired by her husband, concealed her alcoholism from no one but herself. Karen has two younger sisters who both abuse Valium and sleeping pills. Sketched on a sheet of paper, the family dynamics are so nakedly apparent that it takes only a few minutes for Karen to trace the connections. She followed in her father's footsteps, using achievement to gain the high ground and assume the role of the competent, professional, and reliable breadwinner. Gaining her father's approval and adopting his role, all she needed was someone handsome and helpless who would depend on her.

And Bob? His uninhibited style was so attractive that it blinded Karen to everything else. Had she paid attention to his C's and D's in college courses, she might have reflected that he had little interest in achievement. But at the time, that didn't matter. She assumed that she could, in her own words, "train him to be responsible." As long as the thrill ride of romance was on, she didn't have that job. The hard work came later—as it had for her father. In the exuberant early days of romance, Karen wanted one wild ride with a man who seemed fearless, unburdened, and free.

How Do You Pick a Partner?

Why do some personalities attract while others repel? Beyond the insights of poets, is there any explanation for the magnetism that draws you to another person? Sexual attraction is an obvious lure, but how does one person get so invested in another?

In a remarkable book called *A General Theory of Love*, three psychiatrists with widely divergent approaches to their field have produced some fascinating answers to these questions. Thomas Lewis, M.D., is an assistant clinical professor of psychiatry at the

University of California with a background in neuroscience. Co-author Fari Amini, M.D., approaches these topics from a psycho-analytic viewpoint, while coauthor Richard Lannon, M.D., has extensive experience with the use of psychoactive medication to treat emotional illnesses. Pooling their knowledge of psychiatry, the three doctors have focused particular attention on what neurosci-entists call the limbic brain. In their analysis, supported by a con-vincing amount of clinical evidence, Lewis, Amini, and Lannon describe vividly how the limbic brain guides us in making emo-tional choices.

The authors point out that the limbic brain does not have com-plete command over our responses and behaviors; there are two other segments of the brain that also contend for dominance. Obviously, brain function is infinitely complex, and it is impossible to specify exactly which portion of the brain is responsible for each functional choice in your daily life. What fascinates these doctors, however, and what surely confuses all of us (especially when we're falling in love) is what they describe as "the swirling inter-action of the three brains":

> Because people are most aware of the verbal, rational part of their brains, they assume that every part of their mind should be amenable to the pressure of **argument** and will. Not so. Words, good ideas, and logic mean nothing to at least two brains out of three. Much of one's mind does not take orders. . . . A person cannot direct his emotional life in the way he bids his motor system to reach for a cup. He cannot will himself to *want* the right thing, or to *love* the right person.

Emotional attachments are deeply rooted in your early life experiences, and they open up like secret transit maps, channeling your behavior signals through a network of underground tunnels. Emotional attachments cannot be directed or rationalized. They come about as the result of some instinctive, emotional responses deep in the brain that guide you toward some people and away from others. As the authors point out, there is a link between the emotional attachments that are vital to your survival as a child and those that direct and influence your relationships when you're an adult:

> Zeroing in on *how* to love goes hand in hand with *whom*. A baby strives to tune in to his parents, but he cannot judge their goodness. He attaches to whoever is there, with the unconditional fixity we profess to require of later attachments: for better or worse; for richer, for poorer; in sickness and in health. Attachment is not a critic: a child adores his mother's face, and he runs to her whether she is pretty or plain. And he prefers the emotional patterns of the family he knows, regardless of its objective merits. As an adult his heart will lean toward these outlines. The closer a potential mate matches his prototypes, the more enticed and entranced he will be—the more he will feel that here, at last, with this person, he *belongs*.

So every night, Karen accepts a collect call from Bob, who is living at the rehab center in Rhode Island. He lets her know about his ups and downs. In her mind's eye, she still sees the outline of a blond-haired, blue-eyed, cocky and confident Bob—a love image superimposed on the man who needs perpetual care and constant attention.

But gradually, image love is being supplanted by a truer impression of Bob. Karen has started to see how her own comfort system really works. She sees that Bob needs her, just as Karen's mother needed her father, to be steady, sturdy, and supportive. It feels familiar. However difficult to explain rationally, Karen can now see how the situation and circumstances resonate with her limbic needs, how the channels of her brain find a way around her better judgment, and how an uncritical voice takes over. Karen is beginning to understand how Bob's neediness has secured him a place in her emotional life.

Love's Illusions

The limbic brain is a powerful influence on relationships. And if you have performance addiction, some of the characteristics that attract you to a person are probably written into the limbic system.

When you went looking for a partner, did you have certain criteria? If so, what were they? Appearance? Level of education? Professional prospects? Of course, if you don't have a partner and you're looking right now, you can ask yourself the same questions in the present tense. Who is this person supposed to be? What requirements does he or she have to meet in order to qualify as a partner or spouse?

Self-Evaluation:
Is It Image Love or Real Love?

To evaluate your relationship, focus on some of the key questions that will help you understand your attitude toward your partner. These questions should help you define the nature of your relationship.

1. Do you have a history of falling in and out of love easily?

2. Do you fantasize about beautiful women/men as a means of avoiding intimacy with your partner (i.e., "If I could spend one night with him/her, I know I would feel better," or "I hate to admit it, but if she/he looked like so-and-so, I know I could be in love again")?

3. Do you focus on the imperfections of your partner so that you will have an excuse to stay detached (i.e., "If he were not so fat, I would be more eager to sleep with him," or "If she managed the house better, I would want to come home at night")?

4. Do you seldom feel you're able to love the total person?

5. Despite the fact that you have stated your commitment to your partner through marriage or another arrangement, do you feel your love remains superficial?

As you answer these questions, consider what you may be doing to keep yourself from a deeper level of intimacy. If you are fixated on finding the ideal person to love, it's probably because you're searching for a way to avoid your own vulnerabilities.

If you don't resolve your own sensitivities (addressing scene-of-the-crime issues), you're destined to use up a lot of energy trying to fix or perfect others. I have never met anyone who succeeded in healing his or her own hurts by attempting to mold another person into perfection.

Where Are Your Instincts Taking You?

It is quite possible for your instincts to be pushing you toward a relationship where achievement, performance, and appearance are the leading criteria. The result is a marriage that should be perfect. But is it? Some partnerships look good on paper when in reality they never quite work at an emotional level. I think that's exactly the case with Neil and Margaret.

Neil and Margaret: Trying to Make a Marriage Look Right

Neil is the chief financial officer of a major corporation. He and his wife, Margaret, don't have to worry about money. They are the epitome of suburban affluence, and to round out the picture, they have just built a brand-new home in Kennebunkport. They have two young children. "We are a gorgeous couple, and we have gorgeous kids," Margaret told me during her first session.

Margaret works hard to maintain the "gorgeous" part of the contract. At age forty-two, she appears to be in perfect condition. A trim and very attractive woman with large blue eyes, she plays tennis five times a week and lifts weights three times a week.

As her exercise regimen would suggest, Margaret is a person who feels driven by her need to perform. In her own family, she was the youngest of four children. She felt a close attachment to her father, a gifted, affectionate man with a lively imagination, and she was adored by him. With his encouragement she excelled in high school, where she barely dated at all, and as a business major in college.

Her father died in 1992. Three years later, Margaret fell in love with Neil and married him. "Neil was so much like my father—or so I thought," Margaret recalls. "He had that same dry sense of humor."

As their marriage matured, Margaret realized that the resemblance was superficial. Neil turned out to be much more withdrawn and passive than her father. At one point, he told Margaret, "I can never live up to your father. And that's our problem!"

Gorgeous couple. Gorgeous kids. Margaret clings to that image. But this marriage to Neil has become a project, like so many of the other tasks in her life. She got the academic success, the husband, the wealth, the houses, and the children. And now she needs to work full time to make the life inside that picture frame feel as gorgeous as it looks.

It's an extraordinarily tough assignment. Neil has been having an affair with a twenty-five-year-old sales rep. Margaret suspected this for some time, but he initially denied it. She noticed that he was drinking more and more and seemed to be increasingly distant. Then she checked his cell phone records and discovered the truth. Neil has left home and is living with his girlfriend.

Gorgeous family, gorgeous kids . . . but so much fabrication. Margaret has to work out constantly, ignoring the fact that her husband has moved out on her and is having an affair with a younger woman. And now she has to do the additional work of bringing them back together again. That, too, is a personal performance issue. "I think I drove him too much," Margaret tells me. "I expected too much from him. He says he feels inadequate compared to me, and he thinks I am more intelligent than he is. I am, but that doesn't mean I don't love him."

Margaret not only feels guilty for demanding too much of Neil, she also feels responsible for his affair. Margaret wants to save face. If this marriage falls apart, it will be a defeat for her. There is no way she wants to lose this contest.

Does Margaret love Neil? Is that why she wants to save the marriage? Or is this a project taken on by a woman who has performance addiction? Why does Margaret feel so driven to make the marriage turn gorgeous again?

I don't think Margaret really knows. When she went into this marriage, she had the image of what it should be. Now a piece of the puzzle has slipped out of place and she wants to put it back. If she can't, the picture will be ruined.

Is Sex a Performance?

Given the importance of achievement, it's not surprising that sex itself has become a performance issue in many marriages. Expectations of sexual performance are set high. What if you can't meet those expectations? Maybe the problem can be fixed. If an erection is not as reliable as it once was, there's always Viagra. If breasts begin to lose their contours, what about implants? Fat can be trimmed, thighs and buttocks tucked. The right clothing can enhance sexiness, sultriness, power, and mystery. If fantasies lag behind reality, there's easy access to pornography. For psychological challenges, sex therapists come to the rescue. For physical ones, there are lubricants and stimulants. If it's mental, there are uppers and downers.

But all these resources are not much use if performance addiction is interfering with sex between you and your partner. For one thing, sexual intimacy is an expression of uncritical affection. And how can you be uncritical if you are perfecting your own performance while judging and evaluating your partner? If performance addiction is affecting your sex life, you literally lose access to a lot of spontaneous feelings like curiosity, sensuality, and nurturance. The simple human needs for closeness, nakedness, and warmth are abandoned.

BRYAN AND MARY BETH: TRYING TO FIT SEX INTO THEIR PROGRAM

Bryan and Mary Beth have had a celibate marriage for the past seven years. They have a life together. They love each other. What happened? Where did the passion go? Why is their sex life so difficult now?

Mary Beth begins hesitantly talking about last Wednesday night. Like most of her days, on Wednesday every hour was planned. Mary Beth always knew what she wanted to get done.

After dinner, she started to work on taxes. The file drawers were open, receipts piled neatly on the desk, and the computer up and running. Bryan sneaked up on her, put his arms around her neck, and began teasing her. It felt wonderful and she loved it. Before long, he whispered in her ear, "Meet me in the bedroom."

Now, looking back, she can't understand why she didn't. She could have left everything where it was. She would not be arrested, fined, or punished if she finished the taxes on Thursday night instead of Wednesday. But . . .

Here, she loses her train of thought. Listening to her, I can almost feel the power of the forces that have driven her for so many years. She has never been a slacker. When she sets her mind to something, she finishes it. Her gratification comes from a job well done. So . . . she spends a few more minutes with the taxes. And a few more. Bryan doesn't come back. There's no sound from upstairs. In another fifteen minutes, she figures, she will be finished, and then . . .

It was only when she finally came into the bedroom that Mary Beth realized how rejected he felt. She apologized. She tried joking about it—the death and taxes line. But once again they turned in their separate directions and went to sleep. Looking back on that night, Mary Beth realizes what forces were at work. "It was me in this case," she says. "I am so driven at times, I ignore our relationship for the need to accomplish."

As Bryan and Mary Beth explore this sensitive area, they discover that neither is entirely to blame. Bryan is dealing with performance issues of another kind. Knowing that Mary Beth had other lovers before she met him, he has always wondered how he compares to them. She has never said. Should it be an issue? To her, perhaps not, but to Bryan, the evaluation is extremely important. He keeps wondering how he measures up. How does he compare? What's his grade on this report card?

There is much that Mary Beth would like to tell him but not in the evaluative terms of a performance report. She would like him to know that she feels inhibited with him. But she senses the danger in saying this to him. "I'm afraid to tell you what I like or don't like because you're so sensitive about how well you're doing in bed."

Bryan defends himself. Haven't they talked about this? Didn't they tell each other their likes and dislikes? Didn't they talk about those things a long time ago?

I introduce the observation that we all change over the years physically and hormonally and so do our needs for physical contact, affection, and sex. Bryan is not being tested. Mary Beth is not being challenged. Each of them will need words and an open mind to get in sync with each other. Perhaps neither of them is being rejected. Perhaps, after all these years, they can have faith that their love has become a given. Whatever happens in bed, it is not a performance evaluation. They don't have to earn love every day.

What Is Love, Really?

In groups where men and women are talking about their performance addiction, there is a recurrent theme: What is love? The question crosses gender, age, and socioeconomic differences. Surprisingly, it is the question that's asked even by those who grew up in homes where their parents showed affection to each other and their children. But performance addiction can be unrelenting in its demands for comparison, measurement, and competition—and none of these is a component of love.

In romantic love, the question is further complicated by the emotional confusion of passionate sexual relationships. In groups, we have often talked about the binding and blinding effect of sex. Whenever I bring up that phrase, there is general acknowledgment that this effect seems familiar to anyone who has fallen in love.

The binding part is pure physical attraction—lust, raging hormones, and sexual excitement. The blinding component is a screen of illusion obscuring the love object, the partner who is the target of sexual devotion. He or she is not a real person. The partner is a source of escape and ecstasy, an object of desire. When the binding and blinding power of sexual attraction is at its all-time high, one person has no real sense of the dimensions of the other. There are few, if any, flaws and shortcomings.

It's as if the other person's portrait were painted in the boldest of colors that only produce arousal. To really be seen as an individual, the colors need to be toned down and modulated. But it takes time and the maturation of a relationship before the more subtle shades can be acknowledged.

When you are caught up in a binding and blinding sexual relationship, image is everything, and the image produces a magnetic attraction. Only as attraction becomes less insistent do the hot colors begin to cool and you can begin to see the real outlines of the other person.

But when you have a relationship that's been measured in terms of performance, what happens? Is diminishing desire the same as failure? If you have performance addiction, the answer is: Absolutely! As the intensity of a sexual relationship begins to diminish—and inevitably it must—you feel growing pressure to regain sexual prowess.

Needless to say, the job gets harder as you age and as relationships mature. As great sex turns into less-great sex, anyone who's focused on performance begins to ask: "What do I have to do?" In other words, how do you fix this problem and restore the intense sexuality that used to exist?

Then the list begins. Lose twenty pounds. Get a tummy tuck or a breast enlargement. Take Viagra. If you have performance addiction, there's always something you can do. Work out more. Make yourself more glamorous. When you come to the end of the to-do list and those strategies still don't work, what's next?

At the heart of this anxious, energy-draining pursuit is the assumption that the only love worth having is the love that must be won. If you have performance addiction, you may be asking yourself: "How can my partner love me when I have all these imperfections?" Or when you realize your sex life is not what it once was, you begin to analyze what's wrong with your partner and ask, "What do I have to do to get it back?"

These are the wrong questions. An obsessive sexual relationship can live in the imagination, but as a love relationship matures, performance criteria become far less relevant. Human beings are perpetually and stubbornly imperfect. If you have performance addiction, the most unbelievable aspect of love is that you really don't have to pass any test in order to be lovable. There are no criteria. You don't have to do anything special at all to be loved. In fact, you can be loved not just in spite of your imperfections but because of them.

Settling for a Real Person

In a relationship like Mary Beth and Bryan's where sexual spontaneity has turned into an analytical exercise, the strength of loving each other is stronger than the illusion of being wildly in love. And there is a difference.

I turn again to the authors of *A General Theory of Love* for help in defining that difference. Once again, we need to understand the actions of the limbic brain—the part that excites an inexorable and inexplicable feeling of attraction between one person and another. "*Loving*," they note, "is limbically distinct from being in *love*." This distinction, the authors suggest, means that a profound maturation needs to occur if we are to make the transition from being in love to the state of loving.

Loving is mutuality; loving is synchronous attunement and modulation. As such, adult love depends critically upon *know-*

ing the other. *In love* demands only the brief acquaintance necessary to establish an emotional genre but does not demand that the book of the beloved's soul be perused from preface to epilogue. *Loving* derives from intimacy, the prolonged and detailed surveillance of a foreign soul. . . . A culture wise in love's ways would understand a relationship's demand for time. It would teach the difference between *in love* and *loving*; it would impart to its members the value of the mutuality on which their lives depend.

If you have performance addiction, you may find it very difficult to make the transition from being in love to loving. You have to move from a relationship that's fraught with sexual tension and all its expressions—passionate attraction, conquest, and romance—to a state that resembles unquestioned acceptance *by* the other person and *of* the other person. If you love someone, it can feel dangerously close to slacking off or giving up, because there is literally nothing you can do to win love and no criteria you can fulfill to deserve love. Both the giving and receiving are done without qualification.

This realization is more than unsettling; it can actually generate a great feeling of emptiness. If love is unconditional, then what is it that you've been trying so hard to win? If you don't have to pass the test, then what have you been trying so hard to achieve?

When someone who has performance addiction tells me that he or she doesn't know how to love, I suspect it is only half the truth. The other half is that this person does not yet understand how to receive love.

When there's a newfound awareness of the meaning of love, prior assumptions may founder. No one gets exactly what he or she wants in a spouse. So you have to alter your criteria or set them aside if the relationship is going to survive. Ironically, love deepens when your sense of self is enlivened by interactions that do not fit your preconceptions. I think you will feel a little pride when you expand yourself to include the other's differences. When you can acknowledge wishes that deviate from your own, you will discover the true reward of relationships.

All human beings are motivated to obtain love. Yet people with performance addiction often look for other ways to meet an unfulfilled longing. It's when you lose faith in the promise of relationships and substitute performance measures that you become obsessively driven and isolated. Performance addiction often turns a person from promising relationships to an obsessive treadmill of pursuits that have nothing to do with loving.

Of course, we recognize how complicated love can be. One of the biggest challenges is to sort out your feelings so that you can clearly understand your expectations in a relationship. That's where a journal can help. Here are some topics that you might want to reflect upon in the privacy of a daily journal:

1. Describe what factors typically drive you to crave the intensity of being in love (e.g., "I feel like a failure at work," "I've been depressed lately," "My life seems so boring," or "Everyone else seems to accomplish more than I do").

2. Describe what factors typically drive a loss of intensity—the out-of-love stage (e.g., "He or she is not as good-looking as I thought," "He or she is not as wealthy as I thought," or "He or she is not as capable as I thought").

3. If you are in a committed relationship, describe how often you fall in and out of love with your partner, and record the typical factors that contribute to each stage.

4. What does your pattern of involvement and detachment say about your personality? What does that pattern say about your ability to maintain intimacy or your fear of intimacy?

5. Describe the depth of love you witnessed in your parents' relationship. Did your mother love superficially or deeply, with tolerance or with a tendency to criticize? And what about your father?

6. Describe how the parent of the same sex taught you how to love. Did your mother or father expect too much of your other parent? Did he or she seem to love according to what was done for him or her?

7. Asking yourself the same questions, describe how the parent of the opposite sex taught you how to love.

8. Which experiences related to love conditioning are deeply embedded in you? Describe what you have learned in your own family about affection, sexual satisfaction, intimacy, and touching. What function do you think these behaviors served for your mother and father (e.g., protected them from feeling vulnerable, or allowed them to maintain control)?

9. Describe the irrational, emotional learning that has interfered with your ability to love. How has that emotional learning affected your ability to create and maintain intimacy?

10. Do you have the courage to share this information with your spouse/lover? If your defenses are taking over ("I don't need to share this with anyone," or "He or she won't understand"), write down your fears and ask yourself if you're being realistic.

Record the emotions you have been experiencing as you go through this exercise (anxiety, sadness, fear). Most likely, these emotions have interfered with you loving more deeply. Use them as a cue to inform you about your past ("I'm afraid my husband/wife will dismiss my feelings like my father/mother did in their marriage") and to inform you about what you fear in the present ("If I am dismissed, I'm afraid I'll get depressed like my mother/father"). Try to break the impasse and tell your spouse or lover what you have discovered as you've explored these journal topics.

Coming to Terms with Loving and Being Loved

Occasionally, when I am working with a group of men and women who are dealing with performance addiction issues, I will ask them a question that brings them face-to-face with some painful realities: If you and your spouse were meeting for the first time today, would you choose the same partner again? In other words, given what you know, now that image love is long gone, would you make the same choice? And if not, why not?

Their responses tell a great deal about where they are in a relationship. As I have pointed out in an earlier book, *The Power of Empathy,* no marriage is a level road leading to ever-deepening commitment. As we all acknowledge, there are numerous potholes, many ups and downs. But often the level of empathy that we share with a spouse tells a great deal about where the relationship is likely to be headed.

> We go through various stages of intimacy, often bouncing back and forth between the stages on the bumpy but always scenic road called getting to know each other. The first stage is *idealization,* the time when we fall head over heals in love and from that upended position see life in distorted ways. *Polarization* is the second stage, when we move from the idea that everything is "wonderful, perfect, all I ever wanted" to the opposite viewpoint, where we become preoccupied with the little blemishes and flaws in the other person. Noticing all the imperfections, we want to run and hide because those weak spots somehow (we're not quite sure how) seem to reflect back on our own vulnerabilities. . . . From polarization we often make a U-turn and head straight back to the land of idealization, where we begin all over again; or we keep traveling over the potholes and dips in the winding road, hoping that eventually we'll be treated to a smooth ride. With patience, commitment, objectivity, and, above all, empathy, we reach the third stage—*integration.* As our vision expands to encompass the whole picture, we take into account the integrated whole of the other person, which includes both the "good" and the "bad" parts. We learn to see what really matters and let go of what is truly inconsequential.

RICK: LEARNING TO LOVE THE IMPERFECT WOMAN

In visualizing this transition, I am often reminded of Rick, who actually left his wife after many years of marriage only to return later. As he and his wife began seeing each other again, then dating, Rick had the opportunity to reacquaint himself with someone he knew intimately in some respects and yet in other ways not at all. When I asked, "Would you choose her to be your spouse again?" the answer was quite obviously yes, since that was exactly what he was doing. But to that reply he added commentary that provided quite a bit of insight into how their relationship had evolved.

"She's not perfect and *I* certainly am not either, but she is such a good person. She would do anything for her family or mine, and that is important to me. She loves life, and that makes such a difference!"

When Rick was first married, their flawed sex life became the focus of his ongoing disappointment with their relationship. Now, however, Rick has had the opportunity to weigh the sex issues with other qualities in their relationship. "Yes, she is inhibited in bed. She is always unhappy with her body, and in the old days I was, too. I used to obsess about her small breasts, her heavy arms. Now I say, 'Hey, those are *my* arms, *my* breasts, and she loves me.'"

In the past, Rick was wedded to the image of a perfect woman who would be the ideal sexual partner. That has changed. "The perfectionism stuff just doesn't seem worth it. It's all a dream, anyway," Rick observes. "I don't mean I never have lustful thoughts about being with a woman with a perfect body. You know what? My wife probably thinks the same way, about being with a perfect man. But it's just a fantasy. I don't take it so seriously. I guess that means my own view of myself is better."

The process that leads to mature love often threatens couples. As the idealizations wear off, people begin to dislike what they initially appreciated. At a certain juncture, you have a choice to make. You can be open and learn where you need to obtain balance, or you can dig in your heels. But if you dig in your heels, there's a real possibility that you'll reach an impasse.

Clearly, Rick has reached a level of empathy where perfection is just not important. He has gone beyond image love and beyond polarization. Somewhere along the way, Rick has been able to decide for himself what really matters and to distinguish it from the inconsequential. And as that happens, a new life begins to take form. Rick has realized the final stage of a loving relationship: integration.

Daring to Meet in the Middle

As a couple matures to the integration stage of a loving relationship, they need to balance each other. Instead of achieving a perfect relationship, they realize that they need to come to terms with each other and find out what works for them when they're together. It has been illuminating for Eugene and Brenda to see this happening in their relationship.

EUGENE AND BRENDA: MOVING BEYOND RESENTMENT

They aren't married yet but are supposed to be soon, and that's part of the tug-of-war that's going on between them. Wedding plans were postponed once, then again. When Brenda wants to iron out details, Eugene is always too busy.

An analyst in a brokerage firm, Eugene works in an environment where intense criticism is the norm. Totally engrossed in work, he often stays at the office until ten or eleven o'clock, works on weekends, and is anxiously obsessed with his work performance. Initially, Brenda was drawn to him because he seemed so stable and committed

—exactly the opposite of her own father, who was unreliable and emotionally erratic. When she was falling in love with Eugene, she valued his methodical lifestyle. That was her image of who he was.

Eugene saw Brenda as a take-charge kind of person. Brenda worked her way up the corporate ladder, financed her mother's retirement, and provided counsel to her siblings in many ways. She likes to get things done. Initially, Eugene loved her commanding mannerisms, but now that the image love phase of the relationship has lessened, he sees her as too aggressive. Brenda valued Eugene's stability during the image love phase, but she now sees him as chronically ambivalent, fretting over every decision, and always taking an inordinate amount of time before he takes action.

Neither of them noticed these patterns during their early dating. All was wonderful then. But now Eugene resents Brenda taking control and she resents his passivity.

When I told them this is a dilemma that all couples face, it seemed to be a revelation to both of them. And an important one. They are now beginning to understand that they can't stay in the image love phase and that integration needs to occur. If they meet somewhere in the middle, Eugene can have the effect of slowing Brenda down, making her think more before she acts. Brenda can help Eugene take risks and make educated moves without waiting for absolute certainty.

As you read about Eugene and Brenda, does something feel familiar about the process that they're going through? In every relationship, an understanding has to occur if you're going to make it to the higher integration phase of love. Initially, we are drawn to each other to make us more complete people. We are attracted by an aspect of our partner's personality that is underdeveloped in ourselves and very developed in the other. Then we grow to resent the fact that our limitation is being accentuated. Ultimately, the other person's ability is a constant reminder of our deficiency.

But if you and your partner move beyond image love toward integration, you will realize you have something to learn from each other. True, you can't depend on your partner to make up for your own limitations. But perhaps you will become more interested in developing the skill you admire in that person. Achieving that balance, as pragmatic and unromantic as it may seem, just might be the key to eternal love.

What You Can Do about Performance Addiction

At the beginning of this chapter, I asked three questions related to image love. Did you answer yes to any one of those questions? If so, here are some insights that will help you deal with those issues.

Do you find yourself obsessed with a particular trait or physical aspect of another person?

INSIGHT: The next time you find yourself admiring the image of a perfect model or actor, take a moment to figure out why you are attracted to this person. Are you drawn by the beautiful features, the clothes, or perhaps the sexiness or allure of the pose? Identify what is most desirable about this image of the ideal man or woman.

Now think of a moment when you were happiest with someone whom you actually knew. (If you're in a committed relationship, it may be the person you're with now even though you may have lost touch with those happiest moments.) What were the qualities that made you happy? Think of the words that were spoken, the way you touched each other, or the feeling you got when you were in the presence of this other person.

Try to define the similarities and differences between the ideal person in the photograph and the person with whom you were happy. In the real person, was it the pose, the clothing, and the physique that attracted you, or other qualities that made the person desirable and comfortable to be with? Can you separate the truly desirable qualities of the real person from the illusory desired qualities of the imagined person?

Do you feel it is difficult to tolerate physical changes in your spouse or partner as time goes on?

INSIGHT: Physical change is inevitable, of course, but in an empathic relationship, the experience of change is an opportunity for greater intimacy. A woman who is going through the changes associated with aging can ask her husband what it's like for him to see these transformations. What does he find desirable, mysterious, or threatening about the visible changes in her appearance? What about the imminence of pregnancy or menopause? What do these transitions mean to him? How does it change the way he sees her?

For men—who have issues about appearance, strength, and potency—there may be a great need to hide feelings of physical inadequacy behind a protective screen of silence. But trying to explain these physical changes and the emotions that go along with them can go a long way toward empathic understanding. Does his wife still find him attractive if he's balding and over-weight? What if he has trouble getting an erection? What does that mean to her? Does she feel that she's less desirable, or that he can't perform, or that he is somehow failing both of them?

Make sure you talk about these questions. Too often, I find couples resorting to guesswork, innuendo, and implication when sensitive issues about sexuality arise. The opportunities for misunderstanding are vast, leading to greater distance. During pregnancy, for instance, a weight-conscious woman who feels that her body has become bloated and undesirable may not understand that her husband finds her just as sexually desirable or even more so. How would she know unless she asks him and he tells her? Conversely, a man who prided himself on his rock-hard abs may look in disgust at his developing paunch, privately thinking that he's got to shape up. But for whose sake? If he believes his wife will find him less desirable with a paunch and more desirable with rock-hard abs, he may be completely wrong, or half right, or completely right. But he will never know unless he can ask and she can tell him.

Are you more comfortable with your spouse or lover when you are alone than when you're in public?

INSIGHT: Perhaps you wish your spouse had a more impressive title or more status and influence in the community. Or perhaps you are extremely conscious of things that other couples possess—their credentials, their looks, their cars or houses or financial prosperity.

You have choices, of course. You can try to achieve the successful appearance and prosperity of the people who seem to be a whole level above you. But be aware that you may have to give up the comfort you feel with your spouse when the two of you are alone.

How much do you value the comfort that you provide for each other? How important is it? To the extent that you devalue your private relationship and strive for public acceptability, you are likely to find that image love becomes a recurrent issue. Being content with someone and having an empathic connection means that you literally have nowhere else to look and no comparisons to make. As long as you measure yourself against appearances of social attainment and professional achievement, you are placing status above character.

Your spouse or partner will never be able to raise your status in the world or provide you with rewards and accolades that you may need. Only you can do that. But if you can stop looking for these rewards from your partner, you will find the opportunity to receive empathy, understanding, and love. These rewards are not public offerings. They are private gifts achieved through acceptance of the other person rather than the achievement of far-off goals.

Falling in love is easy. True, lasting love always involves knowing the other person. Empathy—the capacity to understand and respond to the unique aspects of another person—is the key to knowing and loving your partner. Ask your partner to do the self-evaluation in this chapter and to write about the journal topics with the idea that you will both share the information. Use this chapter and these exercises as an opportunity to reawaken your feelings toward each other. Periodically revisit your findings and continue to add knowledge about yourself and each other.

6

Exceptional Mediocrity

1. Do you hate the thought of being average in anything you do?

2. Does your mood go up and down depending on how your performance compares to that of others?

3. Do you find yourself labeling others as "less than" when they show imperfections or vulnerabilities?

TO SOME PEOPLE, THE WORD *mediocrity* is literally terrifying. It means you do not rise above the rest. You are no better than anyone else. What is a mediocre person except a faceless being among the masses?

The very essence of the American ethos is a refutation of mediocrity. Our historical mythology is that of a people constantly pushing toward some greater future. We are dreamers and problem solvers. We are rugged individualists and unconventional thinkers. When there are obstacles, we don't let them stand in our way. When we have a goal and a mission, we carry it through to the end. We take what we learned yesterday and build toward a better tomorrow. The trajectory of our lives, like the exploration and growth of the nation itself, is upward and onward. This cannot be called a value system because it has very little to do with values. Rather, it is a way of looking at the world. The world presents obstacles and we shall conquer them.

But if this is the macrocosmic myth, there is also a microcosm of that myth—a day-to-day set of operating principles—that alters our self-perception. For if mediocrity is the ultimate leveler, if it is the antithesis of accomplishment, success, and achievement, how can anyone possibly settle for being average or good enough or just okay? If you depart from the trajectory of success, allowing aspirations to diminish or expectations to collapse, where is your chance at happiness? If you cease to push, dream, aspire, achieve, and accomplish, won't you be miserable?

If you have performance addiction, one indication of this constant striving is how little attention you pay to the regular aspects of self-care and the ordinary gestures that are part of relationships. By self-care, I mean things like daily exercise, nutritious meals, and good sleep habits. By ordinary matters, I mean things like giving your spouse a good morning kiss or saying I love you before you fall asleep at night.

For anyone who fears that mediocrity is the death knell of all human aspirations, there is a terrible reality in living the nonexceptional life. Many people fear brutal disappointment when they speak of giving up or giving in to mediocrity. Instead, they often find remarkable rewards. But the process of finding and accepting those rewards can be so unsettling that it literally requires a change of consciousness and the complete reassessment of an ideology that most of us hold near and dear.

So You Think You're Upwardly Mobile?

Before you can even contemplate the possibility of mediocrity, much less embrace it, take a moment and think about accomplishment. This isn't the same as listing your accomplishments. I'm not looking for an academic record or a resume. What does the word *accomplishment* mean to you?

I think this issue is very *American*. Many of us just accept the notion of upward mobility. If we're not born with a silver spoon in our mouth, we at least deserve the opportunity to get the spoon. This attitude implies that we have the right to strive for accomplishments and achievements, to be rewarded for good performance, and ultimately to end up better off than when we started.

But when you really look at upward mobility, what does it mean? Social acceptance is probably part of it. Some fame or notoriety perhaps, though you can certainly be upwardly mobile without making the social register or being headlined in a national newspaper. When it comes right down to it, we have to admit that most of our commonly accepted indicators of upward mobility are in the form of possessions, income, and professional accomplishment.

When you think about your own life, do you see a ladder in front of you? At some point in childhood, you begin to have a pretty good idea of where you start on the ladder. What's your ethnic background? When did your parents, grandparents, or earlier forebears come to the United States? What did past generations do for a living? In what kind of home and neighborhood did you grow up? Answer these questions and you have some idea of your starting point.

Where does the ladder go from here? For anyone with performance addiction, self-esteem depends on climbing the ladder. And the greater the addiction, the steeper the slope.

PETER: THE LITMUS TEST OF SUCCESS

Peter's father is a Princeton graduate who went on to Harvard Law School. There he graduated third in his class, made law review, and after graduation was immediately hired by a leading New York law firm. After several years, he made partner and became a prominent litigator in the insurance industry. His earnings and investments are in the millions. He has several houses and a yacht. Peter, his only son, graduated from high school and went to technical school for two years to become a building contractor.

Think honestly about this situation. Is it unsettling? Does it make you uneasy? With whom do you identify? Are you thinking it's unfortunate that a son born with such advantages doesn't make it to college, settles for technical school, and becomes a building contractor? Or do you identify with the son? Are you thinking how tough it is that he can't possibly afford the houses, cars, and luxuries that his father has attained? Do you wonder what went wrong because he works in the building trade rather than the professional and financial circles of his father? If you're being perfectly honest with yourself, I think you would have to admit that you automatically assume Peter has taken a step down from his father.

But what else is there to know about these people? Peter's father has been married and divorced three times and is currently in a very unhappy relationship. Peter has a successful construction business and has built up a crew of a dozen men with whom he has worked closely and profitably over the years. Peter's father has always hated the insurance business and got stuck in the law practice because it was lucrative. Peter takes at least a one-month vacation every year with his wife and three children.

Do these factors make a difference? Of course. But how many compensating factors will it take before you sincerely believe that Peter has taken a step up the ladder? My point is simply that the notion of upward mobility—the idea that each generation will do better than the previous one—is so deeply ingrained in all of us that we are ruled almost ruthlessly by the judgments that we make about ourselves and others based on appearances.

Defending Yourself from Mediocrity

In the previous story, Peter and his father are fictional characters. Greg, whose story follows, is not. And because Greg's story is true, it is more complex.

GREG: HIGH STANDARDS, HIGH COST

Sometimes a family builds a virtual wall around itself that protects everyone in that family from the outside world of mediocrity. Within such families, an us-versus-them mentality prevails. We—the family members—set higher standards, hold ourselves accountable, expect more of each family member, and tolerate fewer mistakes. They—the people outside the family circle—may be willing to settle for second best or even shoddiness, but we are nothing like them.

Greg grew up in such a household. His father was a prominent family physician in a small city. The family members along with a few selected friends were allowed to associate with the children. All the children in the family were held to high standards. Greg's father expected absolute compliance with the rules of the household. Meals were well prepared and elegantly served. Each of the four sons had to allocate certain hours for homework when they would not be interrupted. There were no extracurricular activities until schoolwork was done. And when they played sports or practiced musical instruments, they focused on excellence. "There's no point in doing something unless you do it well" was their father's mantra.

In Greg's home, Mom was the silent, efficient, and smiling facilitator. She prepared the meals as her husband wished. She kept the kids to their schedules. When the family prepared for travel, she packed the bags and got everything ready so that they could leave on time.

Looking back, Greg says, "I felt completely isolated. I kept achieving and achieving, and it all meant nothing." But that's his current perception from the distance of many years. My own view is that Greg has probably forgotten something essential about that household. I get the picture of a place where achievement, far from meaning nothing, was actually necessary for survival. What would happen to the children if they failed? What if their grades plummeted, they were late for dinner, or they refused to comply? In a world so clearly divided between us and them—between Greg's family and the outsiders who surrounded them—violations of the unspoken code would have resulted in banishment. Had Greg failed, or defied, or refused, he would have ceased to become one of the exclusive, privileged, and superior members of his family. Instead, he would have been seen as mediocre, undistinguished, and compromised.

In a family responding to the father's perfectionism, the stakes were high. Either Greg could conform, achieve, and win approval, or he could face disdain and the ultimate punishment of indifference. In a world divided between us and them, failure to achieve was sufficient reason for ostracism. Cross the line into the land of mediocrity and there would be no turning back. He lived in an Eden of privilege, but Eden had rules, and exile was the punishment for breaking those rules.

As a boy, Greg stayed on course. He studied hard and got good grades. As soon as Greg showed an interest in gymnastics, his father invoked the mantra of "be all that you can be." His son would be a champion gymnast.

Soon Greg was training every day. He entered competition after competition. He appeared totally dedicated. Following a demanding schedule, Greg practiced to the breaking point. His mind-set was his father's—to prepare for each gymnastic event as if it were his last. Isn't that what it takes to be a champion?

Sure enough, before he finished high school, Greg had a place on the U.S. Olympic gymnastic team. It should have been a triumph. He tried to pretend that it was. But when he looks back on that time, Greg says, "I hated the Olympics. I hated the training, the fear of losing, the fear of my father's wrath. It was never pleasant."

While continuing to train for the Olympics, Greg was accepted at Michigan State. He entered the premed program and seemed destined to have it all. But during Greg's junior year in college, his father committed suicide.

Now, at age forty-eight, Greg looks back on many years that "did not go the way they were supposed to go." After his father died, Greg gave up gymnastics. After all, he had never really enjoyed the sport and had only done it to please his father. He dropped his premed major. That, too, had not been his real interest. His father had wanted him to go into medicine. What was the point of following the lead of a father who had been so dissatisfied with his own life that he had killed himself?

After graduating from college, Greg went into the real estate business, eventually opening a chain of offices through-out western Massachusetts. Yet even though he had apparently divorced himself from everything that could possibly please his father, the same internal mechanisms were still at work. Greg, like his father, could not tolerate mediocrity. He drove himself hard. So what if he could not be a great gymnast or a marvelous physician—he still had to succeed and rise above the rest, which meant staying focused at all costs.

When Greg's twin girls were born, he managed to make it to the hospital. He spent a few minutes in the birthing room. But then he became restless. His wife's labor occurred in the middle of a workday. Greg had some important business to take care of, so he excused himself to find a phone. As his wife was in labor and the twins were being born, Greg was on the phone.

Today, of course, Greg has no idea which business deal took him away from the birthing room, or why it was so important. He does remember that he missed the birth of his daughters. He was physically present but mentally and emotionally absent. The compulsion to succeed had seized him by the throat and would not let him go. Now he wonders how that could happen. Who was he to miss such an important event?

"I was a tyrant to live with," he says, struggling to recognize a portrait of himself. "But," he adds, "everyone in my social circle thought I was great." He was constantly hosting parties. He always seemed to know exactly what to say at the right moment. He was a charmer who could always calculate just how much to influence the next potential client.

His mother, meanwhile, never forgave Greg for not following in his father's footsteps. But Greg had tried to step away from that path when he saw where those footsteps led. The most admired, successful, and important man in Greg's life had in the end been so exhausted or full of despair that he had not even wished to live. And Greg still wonders why. "I believe excellence was his theory of life," Greg observes. "My father finally reached a time when the writing was on the wall. He could not perfect himself, he could not perfect his kids, and he couldn't stand it."

Now that he has made enough money for retirement, Greg wants to feel as if he has climbed to a higher rung on the ladder. He wants to feel secure there, not terrified. Striving hard, he has achieved as much as his father and possibly more. He has discovered that a higher place on the ladder does not make him more confident, satisfied, or fulfilled. Affluence, acumen, social accomplishment, and business success have not delivered relief or release. There is still the danger that the rung might break and he will plunge into mediocrity. After all these years, he still clings to the illusion of "us" as better than "them." Expecting more, demanding more, and being more, the standards are maintained. But what if he lets go?

Accepting the Ordinary

In our group, Greg is just beginning to take the risk of exposing the sides of himself that are weaker, more human, and less estimable—that is, more *mediocre*. The horrible admission of normalcy and the acceptance of himself as an average person with the vulnerabilities and failings of other individuals has not yet crossed his lips. But he says he is working less. He is relinquishing his grip on day-to-day management of the business. He has joined our performance addiction group, where a lot of interactions take place that he previously would have regarded as pointless, stupid, and meaningless.

Among men and women who share many of his human weaknesses, Greg talks about things that had absolutely no place in his steady climb up the ladder of accomplishment. He talks about his family, his childhood, and his emotions. He listens to other people. At first, he tried to figure out why he should be spending time with them—what made them exceptional. But after listening to them and interacting with them, he has allowed at least one barrier to crumble. The similarities are stronger than the differences. They are not exceptional. Neither is he. All his life, Greg has exhausted himself by striving to find differences between himself and "them." At last, he has stopped looking for those distinctions. At great peril to his own self-image, Greg has allowed himself to become one of them.

One day in group, Greg tells us about watching his daughters play soccer. They love it. They play for sheer enjoyment. The last time they were on the field, he stood on the sidelines and just watched them. "They're beautiful—just running and kicking and enjoying themselves!"

Years before, Greg left the room where his children were born so that he could call the office, pick up messages, and contact clients who so urgently needed his attention. This day, watching his daughters happily run up and down the field, he found that he could not tear himself away even for an instant. The enjoyment he got simply from watching them was greater than anything he had experienced in his days as an athlete. As he tells us, he starts to cry. He has truly developed a deepening capacity for empathy—for understanding what naturally brings joy and genuine contentment.

In a family like Greg's where the threat of becoming "like them" is a looming dark cloud, many of the simplest pleasures are stolen before they can be tasted, much less enjoyed. What happens to the joy of gymnastics when it turns into a training exercise? How can hours of play be fully relished when they are seen as hours of waste? What becomes of the imagination when every thought must be measured in terms of accomplishment and every desire directed toward a goal?

If you are struggling with performance addiction, you might want to consider what becomes of people when they are constantly assessed and appraised. What happens if you automatically classify some of those people as supporters of your accomplishments while others are written off as time wasters? Have you preclassified people in terms of those who are exceptional and those who are just mediocre? Not surprisingly, you may find that you have very little patience with human foibles, especially your own.

SELF-EVALUATION:
YOUR TOLERANCE FOR MEDIOCRITY

Your attitudes toward mediocrity, achievement, and competitiveness can be difficult to sort out. Often they are based on unconscious assumptions about yourself and your position in society and the world. The following quiz will help you access some of these attitudes and assumptions. The questions require a yes or no answer. Try to answer as spontaneously and truthfully as possible.

1. Are you ever as great as you want to be?

2. Do you hate the word *mediocre*?

3. Do you have a tremendous desire to be recognized?

4. Do you believe that the most reliable way to win respect is through achievement?

5. Would you absolutely love to be a celebrity?

6. Do you tend to avoid activities if you think you will not excel?

7. Are you very sensitive to being humiliated?

8. Do you constantly evaluate yourself ("How am I doing?") even if the situation is social in nature?

9. Are you privately competing with others even if the situation is noncompetitive (e.g., you attend a wedding and judge everyone's appearance)?

10. Are you more relaxed in a social situation if others seem less knowledgeable than you?

11. Are you more relaxed in a social situation if you think people are less attractive than you?

12. Are you more relaxed if you consider yourself more educated than others?

13. When you enter a friend's home for the first time, do you compare size, amenities, and furniture in that house to your own home?

14. If you make that kind of comparison, do you feel insecure if it's not in your favor?

15. When you go to the gym, do you rate your body compared to others?

16. If you rate your body that way, does your mood fluctuate depending on the rating you give yourself?

17. Have those close to you described you as a driven person?

18. When you make a mistake, do you overreact internally?

19. When others make mistakes, do you feel relieved?

20. Do you feel low if you are with others who are better off financially?

21. Are you very conscious of the type of car you drive?

22. Are you very conscious of the way you dress?

23. Do you rate others according to their possessions (e.g., second home, boat, stock portfolio)?

24. If someone talks about his or her successful job or kids, do you become irritated?

25. Is it very difficult for you to vary your daily routine?

26. Do you find yourself irritated with others who cause you to vary your routine?

27. Are those close to you afraid you will be angry if they ask you to vary your schedule?

28. Do you often wish you could be more spontaneous?

29. Have you been told that your expectations of others are too high?

30. Have you been accused of being too controlling?

31. Have you been accused of being too particular?

32. When you hurt another's feelings, is it difficult for you to say I'm sorry?

33. Have you been told by those close to you that you always have to be right?

34. Do you feel that the love and affection you have from others will diminish if your productivity diminishes?

35. Do you believe you must accomplish certain goals every day to feel worthwhile?

36. Do you seldom make eye contact when walking by others?

37. Do you neglect daily self-care aspects of your life such as nutrition, exercise, and sleep?

38. Do you imagine that those who have achieved greatness are extremely pleased with their lives?

39. Do you have a hard time understanding how some people seem to be so content yet have achieved little beyond average in your eyes?

40. Is it impossible to think of yourself as content if your life remains as it is today?

41. Are you tired of always having to try so hard at everything?

42. Do you feel irritated with the few minutes it took to complete this quiz?

Use the scale below to evaluate your responses to this quiz. This scale will indicate how sensitive you are to being perceived as mediocre by other people. Every yes answer represents one point.

Score (yes answers)	Your sensitivity to being perceived as mediocre
30+	Extremely high
25–29	Moderate
20–24	Average
19 and below	Below average

Accepting Who You Are

Are you completely stuck? Do you feel like you're in a rut where you can't move forward? You might want to look at what's keeping you from the action.

Maybe you're not open to possibilities because you have an unconscious list of standards that are based on preconceptions rather than reality. In that frame of reference, perhaps you are severely limiting the alternatives for your own life by categorizing what's okay for you to do and what's not okay.

TED: CONVINCED HE'S BRILLIANT, SCARED HE'S NOT

Ted is thirty-eight years old, unemployed, and living at home with his mother and sister after a failed three-year marriage. From that thumbnail description, you might make some assumptions about Ted—that he's probably a weak, indecisive guy who can't get it together to find a job, make a decent living, and strike out on his own. But what if I told you that Ted is a Cal Tech graduate? What if I add that he's stubborn, forceful, and strong-willed? Suddenly it seems a lot harder to figure out why he's stuck the way he is.

Here are some more details about Ted that he reveals with hesitation to others in the performance addiction group. He tells us about an incident that occurred when he was twelve. Ted had already been recognized for his academic ability and had skipped ahead a year in school. Sitting in geometry class one day, he faced a tough problem that he couldn't solve. This may not seem like a big deal, but it was for Ted. He started to crumble. Everyone expected that Ted would be able to come up with a solution. After all, he's exceptional; Ted is sure that's the way people view him and value him. If he can't solve this problem and if he isn't really as good as they think he is, what happens to him? He's a big zero, right? He's a fake. He's stupid. He's worthless.

Ted remembers that he burst into tears. There he was, bawling because he couldn't get one geometry problem right. Of course, the teacher was concerned. She asked him what was wrong. Instead of admitting that he was crying because he couldn't solve a geometry problem, Ted told her about his friend whose father was killed in a car accident a few days before.

That story was true. The teacher comforted him, and Ted got a break. He didn't have to face the awful fact that he couldn't solve the problem.

That was twenty-six years ago. Ted now tells us, "In reality, I was more upset with not solving that problem than I was with the death of my friend's father."

So the twelve-year-old had covered up beautifully. All his shame was put into a secret compartment where he hoped it would never be seen. But years later Ted had similar challenges that began his sophomore year at Cal Tech. There were some things he just couldn't get the first time around. Ted was no longer the smartest person in the class.

And then he got hooked. In his junior year at Cal Tech, Ted started experimenting with drugs. He stopped attending classes and got addicted to tranquilizers. By the time the first semester ended, he had failed five courses. He was put on probation. "I would rather fail," he recalls, "than discover that my entire existence was based upon a myth." The myth of infallibility. The myth of smartness. The myth that he was completely different from everyone else around him. What if he was neither a genius nor an exceptionally talented mathematician? In this Cal Tech group, he might be just an average achiever. It was a ghastly thought. Unacceptable. Better to screw up completely than accept that he might be somewhere in the middle. He simply gave up. "I could not stand not being the best," says Ted.

Hindsight provides insight. Ted eventually got his degree from Cal Tech and held a number of good jobs—that is, he was well paid, had challenging projects, and held positions of responsibility. But old patterns die hard. The shame was still a secret. What if he was not as proficient as he thought he was? What if he was just another guy doing another job? Most of the time, he could keep his insecurity under wraps. But when anyone criticized his work or even dared to question it, the doubt triggered an unaccountably powerful reaction. Was his competence being questioned?

Ted responded with rage, which turned into insubordination. In the last job he held, Ted's manager apparently took delight in reviewing Ted's work and pointing out mistakes whenever possible. "He seemed to rely on humiliation as a motivating tool," Ted recalls. Ted took great pride in his reports, spent a lot of time getting them right, and the manager seemed to enjoy picking them apart, especially in group meetings. "The only thing that keeps my sense of self-worth afloat is my work, and he was destroying that every day," says Ted.

Ted's boss put him in a position that made him face his worst fear. "He continually made me mediocre. He was always letting me know that I was just like everybody else."

As the feelings of humiliation became intolerable, Ted's fury increased. One day, after drinking and taking drugs at lunchtime, he stormed into a staff meeting, shouted obscenities at his boss, and embarrassed himself in front of his colleagues. His employment was terminated, and his marriage fell apart shortly thereafter. Ted returned to his mother's home. When he started attending group, he had not worked in over two years.

What prevents him from looking for a job—much less finding one—is the same set of expectations that he has lived with all his life. He fights the battle, but it's a tough one. Throwing himself into the job pool makes him just like everyone else. He talks about the problem he has "working with mediocre people" and "having meaningless conversations." If he tries to rewrite his resume, he finds it never looks impressive enough. The real danger of searching for a job, or getting it, is that he might discover once again that "I am not as smart as I need to be."

Yet Ted is on the verge of change. He has boundless alternatives. But he must first battle the concept of what's okay for him to do and what's not okay. He must deal with his self-perception of an exceptional achiever. He knows the concept doesn't work. It doesn't help him. Achievement has not made him happy and neither has the intentional failure that comes with despair (which is, after all, just another way of proving that he is exceptional—unable to tolerate normal life). Somewhere in himself, in his interactions with the group he has joined, he has the ability to accept his own mediocrity. It is nothing better and nothing worse than Ted accepting himself as a human being.

The Transforming Power of Empathy

In home, at school, and in the workplace, most of us experience a lot of testing, measurement, and evaluation. Naturally, this nurtures an image of hierarchy based on performance and achievement. To parents who evaluate their children, the high achiever seems more of a gift and less of a headache than the low achiever. To teachers in the classroom, the A students are surely more highly regarded than the D students. In the workplace, the highly efficient and intensely persistent employee is the most likely to be rewarded and promoted. All these incentives reinforce our perception that people who are average or mediocre on these scales of measurement are less admirable and less worthy than those who excel.

Unfortunately, there is no sliding scale that can measure the extraordinary power of empathy. This quality represents one of the truest successes in life. Of course, I don't mean success in terms of financial rewards or career accomplishments. I am referring to the kind of success that makes the experience of day-to-day life a lot richer. And empathy can show up in the most unexpected places.

Sylvia: Taking the Time to Understand

My contact with Sylvia, a sales representative for a high-end stereo manufacturer, started out with a very minor household issue. In our family home we have one stereo made by this company; often my daughters, my wife, and I compete for it. When one of my daughters is home, she likes to have it in her room. I take it to the cellar for a workout. My wife likes it in the family room.

One Sunday morning, I was reading an ad in *Parade* magazine about an acoustic stereo made by the same company that was larger and supposedly had a better sound. I called the 800 number. I reached a saleswoman in North Carolina and asked a few questions. She was delightful. After she asked me to repeat my name again, she commented that she remembered talking to my wife four years earlier when we ordered the first stereo.

That stirred my curiosity. How could she remember a conversation that had occurred four years ago? We talked for a bit about her memory before I got to my reason for calling. I asked about the larger version of the stereo that I'd seen advertised. Sylvia asked me the size of the rooms where we were using the radio, particularly the family room. When I said I didn't know, she suggested that I could measure the largest room and give her the square footage. Then she could be of further help.

My wife and I took the measurements, and I got back on the phone. Sylvia commented that it was probably not necessary for us to have the larger version of the stereo in our home. But when I mentioned that the family room had a cathedral ceiling, she said she thought the sound would be better on the larger stereo, so we ordered it.

A simple, everyday transaction. How did it involve empathy? Empathy is everyday mind reading. It's the ability to accurately assess another person's point of view. Empathy always accents finding out the facts. It is objective (as opposed to sympathy, which is subjective). Sylvia displayed warmth. She was trying to ascertain the facts. And she was making a positive relationship by remembering my name.

It could have been an average interaction between a customer and a telephone sales representative. And in many respects, it was. I inquired about a product, and I got the answers I needed. The quality that made that interaction exceptional and turned a straightforward transaction into a memorable encounter with a good human being was simply an added element of empathy.

Being Stuck

Let's return to the issue of being stuck. But this time, ask yourself whether it has something to do with your concept about who you are and what it's possible for a person like you to be doing.

First, look at the imagined ladder of progress. Do you expect that you have to outperform your parents, or at least meet their expectations in terms of rising in the world? That may seem like a given, but when you look closely at those expectations, I'm sure you'll discover that they set unnecessary limits. Look at the story of Peter. If your parent or parents have been professional achievers, what does it mean if you're not? If your parents made a great deal of money, what does it mean if you make a lot less? What if your home is smaller and your possessions fewer?

Are you already saying to yourself, "I'd be settling for less"? If so, congratulate yourself because you've identified part of the trap. That "less" is in terms of prestige, position, and accomplishments. But less in terms of satisfaction? In terms of happiness in your relationships? In terms of day-to-day contentment?

For Greg, it took his father's suicide to jolt him into an awareness that the preordained path up the next rung of the ladder held more despair than promise. From there, he could begin his own search. But Greg's story illustrates another dilemma. Even when he struck out on his own, he could not shake off the feeling that he had to be better and separate from others. His sense of self-esteem could not tolerate an environment where he was just like everyone else. Though he chose a different route, Greg, like his father, had to drive himself. He always felt as if opportunities were waiting for him just around the corner, and if he neglected those opportunities, he would be breaking some kind of contract with destiny.

So ask yourself: How great is the danger of mediocrity? What if you are no better than the person sitting to your right and no worse than the one to your left? If you have been striving to achieve and all it gets you is a place in the middle that leaves you feeling empty, then it's no wonder you're hooked on achievement. For performance addicts, the absolute need to be exceptional is so tied in with the requirement of performing exceptionally that the two seem inseparable.

Now do an exercise in your own mind where you try to differentiate your need for achievement from your needs for love, respect, and self-esteem. This may be hard work. As I have pointed out, our instructions to achieve come not only from teachers and parents; those instructions are deeply embedded in the American social structure. You have to make a leap of faith to believe that you will be worth a great deal even if you do not take a single step up the ladder of social mobility. That leap begins with saying, "I am not the highest achiever, or possibly not even a high achiever."

Remember, accomplishment is worthwhile when your drive comes from a genuine place within. If you're trying to soothe your insecurities through joyless achievement, you will defeat yourself every time.

If you can't be measured by your achievements, how can you begin to find a way to value yourself? We will explore this question in subsequent chapters. For now, take a few moments to explore the things you can do. This is an opportunity to begin playing with possibilities to help yourself go beyond the boundaries that you may have unconsciously set. It's the next essential step in overcoming performance addiction.

What You Can Do about Performance Addiction

The three questions that I posed at the beginning of this chapter are directly related to issues of self-image and attitudes about mediocrity. If you answered yes to any of those questions, I urge you to complete the short assessment below. It could have a significant impact on decisions you make in the future. Be sure to finish all five steps and keep the lists you make. These are important issues, and you may want to return to them later.

1. List five things that give you the most enjoyment and pleasure in your daily life. You can be as imaginative as you want with this list—for instance, unlimited vacation and travel or unlimited time with your children. Title this your "Pleasure List."

2. Now list five great accomplishments that you would like to have on your resume. (It's fine to list the Nobel Prize or as much money as Bill Gates.) Title this your "Accomplishment List."

3. Compare the two lists. Think what would happen if none of the great accomplishments ever ended up on your resume. Suppose someone guaranteed that you'd never attain those accomplishments? How could you pay more attention to the things that give you enjoyment and pleasure?

4. Now let's look ahead, based on the assumption that you can't get anything that's on your Accomplishment List. Return to the Pleasure List and assign a number from 1 to 5 to each of the items on that list (the first item is the most important).

5. As a final step in this exercise, write down one thing that you will do tomorrow to enjoy the first item on your Pleasure List.

7

The Lure of Glamour

1. Have you been wishing to be drop-dead gorgeous or extremely handsome most of your life?

2. Have you hated one or more of your body parts most of your life?

3. Do you believe that if you could change those body parts, your life would be dramatically different?

4. Do you weigh yourself daily?

5. Are you intolerant of weight gain?

6. Are you intolerant of the aging process?

IF YOU'RE A WOMAN, you're statistically much more likely than a man to answer yes to most or all of these questions. But why?

Aren't women judged by their looks more often than men, and don't those judgments have far-reaching implications in all aspects of their lives? What about the models of attractiveness and femininity that constantly remind women of what they could or should be? Isn't it obvious that those images are pervasive? Women who are extremely thin are often envied.

For women, the competitive and sometimes compulsive striving for self-improvement in terms of appearance is often the most

outright evidence of performance addiction. The process of beau-
tification is frequently experienced as the pathway to love and
acceptance. Striving for perfection becomes translated into a need
and desire to attain some impossible standard of beauty. Finding out
how to become attractive, then doing everything to attain that
ideal, can become an addiction as powerful as any narcotic.

Anorexia and Performance Addiction

The problem of anorexia, particularly among teenage girls, has
been equated to an epidemic in recent years. It is a complex illness,
with many contributing psychological factors, and there are no
easy answers for this complex and sometimes fatal illness. But I
believe it is worth looking at some of the subconscious factors that
contribute to anorexia, as they apply to many women who allow
issues of self-image to dominate their lives.

One component is certainly perfectionism. The good body is
never good enough. If you have anorexia, some trace of fat can
always be found somewhere. There is constant internal fault finding—a systematic search for what's wrong. Put-downs and self-
derision are automatic. "Why am I so fat?" and "Why am I so
ugly?" are the mantras. It's useless to reassure the anorexic patient
by insisting that she is neither. Accepting her body just as it is
would constitute a kind of defeat. Her internal message is "I must
do better."

Another component is certainly the desire to please. We often
find that anorexic girls are excellent students and obedient children
eager to follow the wishes of parents and teachers. In adolescence,
there is the added component of wanting to please boys. The
anorexic girl hopes to be so slim and attractive that she could
never be considered fat.

With any kind of eating disorder, secrecy is also an important
component. To her girlfriends, the anorexic may constantly talk

about eating too much, feeling too full, putting on weight, or wishing she looked like so-and-so. But if she is actually starving herself, she will usually try to hide it, then deny it as long as possible.

Finally, there is a consistent unreality about what she looks like, how she feels, how others perceive her, and what she will gain by achieving the ideal body that she's seeking. Parents and friends of girls with anorexia soon learn that there's nothing to be gained from praising her appearance or reassuring her that she is just as slim and attractive as anyone could wish. To someone with anorexia, compliments are empty. When she looks in the mirror, she actually sees a fat person. She sees someone who is distasteful-looking or ugly. Why would anyone want to associate with her? How could anyone pretend that they don't see how awful she really looks? Her self-image cannot be enhanced with encouraging words. The girl she sees in the mirror bears no resemblance whatsoever to the person seen by her friends and parents.

It could be argued that many of our distortions—like our images of beauty—are culturally based and are the result of social convention rather than any absolute standard of measurement. For society as a whole, that is certainly true. A beautiful woman in today's commercial representations is a far cry from the perfect beauty that Rubens once glorified in his famous nudes. Today, the graphic models of perfection tend to be anorexic women. But what we call eating disorders have more to do with perceived imperfections than with any actual standard of beauty or perfection. Being thin is a particular fixation because it is a way of insisting that "I'm not good enough" and "I'm not desirable enough." But if it were not the weight issue, it would be something else. Wanting to be more beautiful is just a compulsion.

The Notorious Thinness Industry

Performance addiction is especially rampant in the world of high-profile celebrities and models, where weight loss has become the all-consuming measure of acceptability. Turn to the image-obsessed pages of *Cosmopolitan* magazine and an October 2002 article on "Incredible Shrinking Stars" provides statistical evidence of what any viewer can see with the naked eye. Stars are fiercely and desperately competing to shed weight now. Looking at before-and-after shots of such models of perfection as Julia Roberts, Jennifer Connelly, Selma Blair, Christina Ricci, Brittany Murphy, and Mena Suvari, the dietitian Julie Walsh estimated that each of these stars had lost at least ten to fifteen pounds in the previous two years.

In Hollywood, where anything over a size six is overweight, the average size has dropped from a size four to a size two. Even so, a trainer to the celebs, Michael George, says actresses who want to lose another two or three pounds are constantly coming to him. He looks at them and tells them it's not possible. They don't want to hear it. "Being underweight can be physically damaging and emotionally draining, since dieting can be as addictive as any drug," George told *Cosmo*.

Adrienne Ressler, a body image expert at the Renfrew Center, an eating disorder treatment facility in Fort Lauderdale, Florida, has noticed that when an actress is lauded for looking healthy or looking great, she's likely to take it as an insult. "'You look too thin' is the compliment," says Renfrew.

It's no secret that millions of American women, especially young women, compare themselves with these celebrities. And there's a direct and obvious link between these models of perfection and the diet-addictive behavior of many teenage girls who are literally starving themselves. It is another facet of performance addiction—they need to achieve a physical manifestation of acceptability that will in some way compensate for the feeling of not being good enough.

No body is ever perfect enough, so the incessant search for physical perfection leads to infinite disappointment. Often the need for approval leads to an equally futile quest to find the perfect man to validate a sense of being wanted and needed. Inevitably, the quest results in the disappointing discovery that the perfect man is just as flawed as other human beings.

The Compulsion to Conform

The actual method of acting out, whether losing weight, developing a sculpted body, or getting cosmetic surgery, is really an expression of the compulsion rather than a realistic and truthful response to the social and cultural environment. Of course, people care about appearances. But no one is asking you to almost kill yourself so that you can look great.

How far are you willing to go to change your appearance? That question is not a test for anorexia or any other eating disorder. Rather, it is a way to begin talking about what's motivating you to meet certain standards or expectations and to discover what you're really after.

For someone with performance addiction, there's really no such thing as reaching a weight goal or a fitness level that can feel satisfactory. When you have performance addiction, being five pounds lighter only means that you can lose another five pounds, or that you must work harder to maintain the weight loss you've already achieved. All the signs of aging such as sagging skin, wrinkles, and hair loss are challenges to be met with a full arsenal of resources. Beyond the gym, the hairdresser, and the cosmetologist, there are personal trainers, dermatologists, and plastic surgeons—a whole range of professionals who stand ready to join ranks with you in the battle against the years. For performance addicts, it is unthinkable to give in, which would be the equivalent of giving up.

But what will you gain if you maintain an unrelenting and unforgiving campaign to stay in the best shape possible? And perhaps more to the point, what will you lose by doing so?

The Signs of Workout Addiction

There is a pervasive myth in our culture that, by perfecting our bodies, we can rid ourselves of the insecurities that have plagued us all our lives. How ironic that in our efforts to be perfect, we begin a process that can erode our health and leave us with an addiction rather than a cure.

Roseanne: Workouts and Self-Esteem

At age fifty, Roseanne is obsessed with exercise and weight loss. She gets up at 4:30 every morning and works out for two hours before getting ready for her public accounting job. In the evening, she spends another hour in the gym. For three years, she has been on a high-protein diet that initially helped her lose weight and now, in her view, gives her all the nutrition she needs to maintain her stringent exercise schedule without regaining weight. If she misses a single workout, she starts to become anxious and frustrated. No matter why she missed the workout, she blames herself for negligence and closely examines her motives. Is she starting to fall back into her old ways? Could it be that she's losing interest or that her strength of will is beginning to fail? Thus, a missed workout for Roseanne is more than that—it's the first step on a slippery slope that leads straight to dissolution and disaster. Once she loses her focus, she fears she'll never regain it.

During one of our sessions, I begin to talk about the potential downside of too much exercise. She contemplates cutting back on her schedule but wants me to guarantee she won't gain weight if she does cut back. "I just *can't stand fat*," she says. "I would rather be crippled than gain the weight back."

In fact, she may already be making the choice. A bone scan has revealed that she has osteoporosis. Certainly, three years on a protein diet has done nothing to enhance bone strength, since excessive protein depletes calcium. But the thought of reducing her regimen and returning to a normal diet is anathema to her.

A phobia of fat? An obsession with weight loss? Or a relatively normal and realistic reaction to signs of aging? I wonder aloud why there's so much at stake for her in continuing to work out at such an obsessive level.

We don't have far to look. Roseanne's father died when she was seven years old. After that, she lived with her mother, two older brothers, and younger sister. None of them was able to talk about the death of their husband and father, but Roseanne's mother immediately began to put on weight, "eating away her grief" until she was obese. The brothers never said a word to their mother but instead picked on Roseanne, taunting her for being overweight and unattractive (she was neither). Her sister, four years younger, escaped the torture. The brothers only picked on Roseanne, telling her that no boy would ever like her. Roseanne fought back, but the message was implanted in her consciousness.

Roseanne has never been married and is now living with Bruce, who owns an insurance company, drinks too much, works too hard, and constantly brings Roseanne back to the scene of the crime. All it takes is a critical word about her appearance to send her anxiety soaring again. If she doesn't meet Bruce's expectations, will he disappear the way her father did?

Roseanne has experienced men as either critical or absent and has the image of her obese mother eating her way out of her grief. No wonder she faces her workout schedule as if it were a life-or-death issue. No wonder she would rather be crippled than fat.

For Roseanne these are more than matters of appearance. They are issues that get to the very root of the way she values herself as an individual. With fat comes invisibility and feelings of worthlessness. The workouts are indeed work. But performance addicts will fully appreciate why Roseanne believes that the work is necessary for self-esteem. As long as she is counting repetitions, improving on yesterday's results, moving faster, and lifting more, Roseanne feels temporary relief from anxiety. This is what she needs for survival. With achievement, she is released for a very brief time from the yawning uncertainty of self-doubt.

Do You Exercise by Choice?

You may be wondering whether I'm saying that everyone involved in a weight-loss program is a performance addict. You may argue that statistics show many Americans need to lose weight for health reasons. Further, it can be easily proven that both men and women who maintain a reasonable weight are more likely to have a positive body image and therefore have improved self-esteem.

Of course, I'm not about to argue with any of that. The health risks of obesity are well recognized, and we know that people who are severely overweight are more likely to have problems with social confidence and self-esteem issues. Even income is affected; people who suffer from obesity earn less on average than those who maintain a normal or controlled weight.

But the obsession with weight loss that's linked to performance addiction is based on unrealistic standards of achievement or self-discipline rather than any real benefits related to health or self-image. For a performance addict, the fixation on exercise and dieting is an obsession with a goal that can never be achieved, rather than a reasonable objective like good health. If you're happy with an exercise and nutrition program, you can feel better without using a scale or tape measure to tell you that you are better. In an obsessive program, however, results are constantly measured, criteria are ever more demanding, and perpetual failure is virtually guaranteed.

When Looking Good Is Never Good Enough

Concern about looking more attractive may begin as a wish for acceptability, but it often blossoms into a frantic search for identity. Among my patients, there is no better example of this search than twenty-four-year-old Kristy. Her personal history leaps across cultures.

KRISTY: EXPECTATIONS IN TWO DIFFERENT CULTURES

Kristy was born in Japan and lived there until age sixteen. Her family came upon hard times when she was three years old, and she had to move in with her grandparents, who took care of her until she was five. She then moved in with her mother, seeing her father only occasionally between the ages of five and eight. He was gone on two-month trips, rarely returning home. "I had no idea what he thought of me," Kristy recalls. "I would cry and cry when he would visit, beg him to stay, and then he would disappear again and be gone for what seemed like years."

When her father finally returned to live with the family, Kristy found him to be a hard taskmaster. He helped her with her studies, particularly mathematics, and Kristy remembers how he would hit her over the hands when she failed to understand something. "He told me it bothered him to hit me," she says, "but he said he had to do so, to make me learn better."

When the family moved to Los Angeles, her parents found jobs in the hotel business. Her father was disappointed in himself, bitter that he did not strike it rich in America, but his ambitions for his daughter grew by leaps and bounds. "He wanted me to be attain more and more. He would not be satisfied until I got my Ph.D. In Japan, the only way a girl can make it is to be super bright, get to university, and excel."

But they were no longer in Japan, and Kristy began to hear messages that were very different from those of her parents. "I always thought *being smart* was everything. Then I come to the States, and the only thing anyone cares about is how I look. I never even *thought* about how I looked when I was in Japan."

Now Kristy finds that she constantly struggles with the demands of both cultures: the demand from her Japanese father that she be intellectually perfect and the demand from her American peers for physical perfection. Her life has become a constant exhausting struggle to satisfy both. She got her bachelor's and master's degrees from UCLA and is working on her Ph.D. At the same time, she has become very American by calling herself fat, not pretty enough, and less than desirable.

It is no exaggeration to say that Kristy is wearing herself out. The pressure is relentless. When she is at school, she has to be exceptional. When she is with friends hanging out, shopping, or going for a run, she evaluates herself to make sure she is saying and doing the right things. By the time she heads home at night, she is so exhausted that all she wants to do is "crash and eat junk food." She stops at the corner grocery store. "I get so disappointed in myself. I buy junk and I know all the while that I am doing the wrong thing. But I just need relief—no more pressure!"

No wonder she is exhausted! Kristy's cross-cultural background is a perfect setup of compulsive demands in two cultural languages. Her disappointed immigrant parents have transferred all of their own frustrated ambitions onto their daughter. Her American friends have thoroughly indoctrinated her with peer pressure expectations that she should be slimmer, more attractive, and more desirable. And the catalyst is Kristy herself—a personable, attractive, and warm person with a strong sense of personal and social responsibility.

Ironically enough, Kristy did not start therapy with feelings of rebelliousness, resentment, or anger. Initially, she could not even bring herself to complain of exhaustion. She was so intent on being good, doing well, and appearing together that she would not think of complaining about her career, friends, or lifestyle much less her parents or family. What brought her to my door and from there to the group was a far more puzzling dilemma. She was attracted to two men and both were attracted to her as well.

And the dilemma? Neither of them, as far as she could tell,

measured or evaluated her by any of the standards with which she was familiar. Neither seemed particularly concerned with whether she got a Ph.D., was an exceptional mathematician, or had a promising career. Neither was critical of her appearance. Though each of the men was quite different, and though she liked both of them, the fact that they liked her for no discernible reason was utterly confusing.

Never had Kristy imagined a universe in which she could be appreciated and accepted for who she was rather than how she performed. It was as if her whole world had been turned upside down.

What Are Your Reasons?

If you are trying to change your appearance, I would simply ask why. What will you gain if you come closer to achieving the image that you would like to attain?

As I've indicated, I know there are perfectly valid reasons for changing to a healthful diet or losing weight. Weight control is a major factor in preventing heart disease and diabetes, and dietary choices influence a wide range of other chronic diseases from gout and arthritis to liver and kidney conditions. To achieve those health benefits, there are numerous dietary changes that you can incorporate into your lifestyle and a great variety of sports and athletic activities that can contribute to cardiovascular health and help prevent bone problems and joint disease. But those are actual benefits that can be achieved by making a transitional shift to a healthier lifestyle.

Are those the benefits that you hope to achieve? Or is something else driving you? You might wonder why it's important to make a distinction. What does it matter whether you diet and work out to create a more perfect body image or whether you do it for health reasons? Why examine the motives and motivations when you really want to focus on results? The difference is radical both in terms of the impact on your body and on your psyche.

It's illuminating to turn to the recent work of Robert Thayer, Ph.D., particularly his book *Calm Energy: How People Regulate Mood with Food and Exercise*. Thayer points to surveys showing that many people are no longer exercising as a way to feel better or improve their health. In fact, he cites a *Psychology Today* survey indicating that 24 percent of women would actually sacrifice three years of their lives if they could only be the weight they desired. Thayer also explores ample evidence that for all our concentration on diet and fitness, the number of overweight Americans has steadily increased over the past twenty years.

What lies behind these statistics? Thayer makes the persuasive argument that more of us turn to exercise as a way to relieve stress rather than relishing the pleasures of activity and the health benefits that exercise can confer. "Our collective mood is worsening," Thayer concludes, as evidenced by the sharp rise in clinical depression and related problems such as violence, drug use, and suicide. Surveyed about the degree of stress in their daily lives, 14 percent of Americans in the 1980s said it was a significant factor. By the 1990s, that number had risen to 18 percent.

Are you exercising because you enjoy it, feel better, and appreciate its benefits, or because you hope to burn away stress, lose weight, and firmly discipline yourself? For the person who is able to enjoy exercise, there is a reward in the form of what Thayer calls "calm energy." For someone who has performance addiction, however, the calmness is rarely achievable. With performance addiction, a person may exercise steadily, furiously, or methodically, but what drives that person are forces that feel beyond his or her control. Exercise, like dieting, becomes a compulsion. And the outcome is not greater energy or more enjoyment of life—the end result is exhaustion.

Giving Yourself a Reprieve

If you are feeling stressed out and fatigued, it might be your own highly critical self-voice that's helping to drive you to exhaustion.

Kelly's story is typical of many in that she found herself becoming her own most ardent and implacable critic. Even when she tried to get away for a hard-earned break, that self-voice would give her no peace.

KELLY: ATTACKING HERSELF FOR HER LOOKS

Kelly has just returned from vacation. Think vacation, and what comes to mind? A break from work, certainly. A chance to get away from the stresses and strains of home and work-place, to kick back and relax. Vacations aren't perfect, of course. But they're a wonderful opportunity to escape from the usual routine.

That's not how it was for Kelly. "I put on this two-piece bathing suit and saw myself in the mirror, and I couldn't believe it. I'm so fat! My butt sticks out!" When she talks about eating, it's in terms of "pigging out," "gorging," and "stuffing myself." Then she goes on to talk about her skin problems—the wrinkles, the blemishes, the cellulite.

Whatever happened on that vacation, it was certainly not calming and enjoyable. I ask Kelly to desist from name-calling and try to find the roots of her intense reactions. Going back to the scene of the crime, she recalls how her parents focused on her body and how self-conscious she was about not looking right. Even today, when she visits her parents, she knows they will critique her on whether she looks skinnier or fatter, older or younger. They will freely share their opinions about what she's wearing, and if they disapprove, they'll let her know it.

"But I can't keep blaming my parents," she says. True. But she is not blaming them. She is, in fact, taking their side. When she calls herself names—"fat," "flabby," and so on—it's as if she is doing her parents' work for them. She anticipates their worst criticism almost as a self-defense. If she can get there before them by criticizing herself and her appearance, perhaps she can arm herself against their remarks. Her best defense is an attack on herself.

So much for Kelly's vacation. When she goes back to the gym and begins working out again to get rid of the "fat" and the "flab," she will not enjoy the exercise. As she has done since girlhood, she will be trying to gain acceptance. The exercise is not a reward. Rather, it is a punishment for not looking right and not being right. As she pedals, lifts, and runs to lose weight, improve muscle tone, and erase excess fat, she is subconsciously reaching for an impossible goal. If she succeeds, she will be acceptable at last.

But of course she can never succeed. The more she works to become flawless, the more stressed she becomes. All the pent-up feelings from the constant critiquing turn to a kind of frenzied name-calling, then to a burning desire to push harder, run faster, and press harder so that she will be loved at last. Frustration is inevitable because the goal cannot be achieved this way. Whether or not it is ever possible for Kelly's parents to love her just as she is, one thing is certain: More workouts and more dieting will not bring her any closer to getting the respect, acceptance, and love that she wants. She just can't quite believe that she deserves these emotional rewards because of who she is rather than what she does.

How to Get What You Want

Why do you work out? Why do you diet? What do you hope to attain? If you have set your sights on benefits that are truly achievable or if you simply enjoy what you're doing, you're far more likely to find yourself in a state of calm energy where enjoyment comes from the doing. But if the search for a more glamourous body leads you to intense, stressful competition not only with others but also with yourself, perhaps you need to see whether your actions are bringing you any closer to the outcomes you want to achieve.

Following are some writing exercises that will help you discover important information about how you see yourself, how others see you, and how you relate to issues like dieting and exercise. I believe there are close links between performance addiction, relationship avoidance, and attitudes about weight and appearance. The writing exercises will help you make some of those connections and better understand how attitudes toward body image are affected by your relationships with people. Remember that how you manage relationships is directly correlated to how you view your body. If you communicate poorly with others, you are providing fuel for your performance addiction.

What You Can Do about Performance Addiction

At the beginning of this chapter, I asked six questions to help you evaluate your issues about body image and appearance. If you answered yes to any of those questions, I recommend the writing assignments below. Each assignment is designed to help you address a specific issue related to a specific question. The goal of this writing assignment is to move your own attitudes in a positive, realistic direction.

Have you been wishing to be drop-dead gorgeous or extremely handsome most of your life?

WRITING ASSIGNMENT: Ask one or more people who are close to you to give you an honest appraisal of your physical appearance. Write down exactly what they say and compare their descriptions to your typical view of yourself.

Ask the same person or persons to give you a fair appraisal of your personality and your character. Again, write down what they say and compare their views to your own.

Finally, write about your relationship with this person (or these people), weighing what's most important about your interaction.

Evaluate how much of this relationship depends on appearance factors and how much depends on personality and character factors. *Have you hated one or more of your body parts most of your life?*

WRITING ASSIGNMENT: Write down the last time your self-voice was filled with negative labels such as "I'm so stupid; I'm so ugly; I hate how fat I look." Have you noticed that you focus on your dissatisfaction with your body as a means to avoid conflict with others? Go back and discover what interactions preceded this labeling. Repetitive name-calling is often a means of avoiding expressing yourself to another person. Essentially, it is a lack of faith in your ability to manage conflict successfully, so you try to solve problems by perfecting yourself. For instance: "If I perfect myself physically, I won't have to deal with any conflict with my partner, lover, boss, etc."

Do you believe that if you could change those body parts, your life would be dramatically different?

WRITING ASSIGNMENT: When you see yourself in a full-length mirror, are you accepting, rejecting, tolerant, disgusted, or realistic about what you see? Describe how you learned to view yourself in this manner. Initially we learn to see ourselves through other's eyes. Now try to be objective as possible: describe the absolute truth of what you see, unbiased by other people's expectations and prejudices. Write a new description.

Do you weigh yourself daily?

WRITING ASSIGNMENT: Describe how your attitude toward food affects your experience of eating. Does it spoil the joy of tasting good food or satisfying your appetite? Then describe your experience with exercise. Do you do it for the joy of using your body, for your health, to alter your physique, or to burn fat?

Review your insights on eating and exercise and evaluate which of your answers are signs of performance addiction. Then write about the experience of a person who has a healthy sense of self. Identify what you consider to be a joyful view of exercise. Describe what it's like to enjoy a meal without dwelling on weight gain or body fat. As you describe those experiences with eating and exercise, try to live them in your own mind as well.

Are you intolerant of weight gain?

WRITING ASSIGNMENT: Describe the greatest sensitivities you have in interactions with others. Describe the most difficult experiences to put into words. (For example: "I can't let anyone know when I am really angry," "I can't ever tell anyone that I am disappointed in them," or "I can't say what I like and don't like sexually.") Record your eating and exercising habits after you have avoided one of these interactions. As you're writing about this topic, see if you can discover the connection between your body-weight issues and the way you express yourself with other people.

List the promises you typically make to yourself regarding food. (For instance: "I won't eat potato chips today" or "I am not going to eat ice cream all week.") Describe how you feel when you break your promise. Are you harsh with yourself? (For example: "I'm such a loser!") Are you understanding with yourself? (For example: "I shouldn't have eaten the ice cream, but it is summer and it's unrealistic to think I won't eat ice cream at all. I am going to stop bringing it into the house, though. I realize with the work pressure I have now, I am turning to sweets to cope.") Describe what reasonable people would say to themselves when they eat what they have told themselves to avoid.

Are you intolerant of the aging process?

WRITING ASSIGNMENT: If there's one thing you know for sure, it's that the clock will move forward. This writing exercise can help make you feel more tolerant toward a process that's inevitable.

Rate the priorities in your life—for instance, your work, love relationships, friendships, family relations, parenting, and appearance. Then review this rating list and look at how much importance you have given to appearance. Consider the conscious choices you would have to make to give less weight to glamour issues and put more emphasis on other aspects of your life. Describe how you would like to deal with appearance issues, then describe how you will move in that direction.

8

The Quest for Glory

1. Does your work title lack the prestige you really desire?

2. Do you find yourself constantly calculating how much money you are making?

3. Are you easily impressed by another person's credentials?

4. Do you tend to idealize those who have power, regardless of their character?

I'M SURE THERE ARE MANY women who can answer yes to all or some of these questions. But among performance addicts, I've found that far more men than women are struggling with issues related to status, income, dominance, and respect.

Not surprisingly, there is considerable evidence that the relentless pursuit of dominance is hardwired into the male psyche. In a series of experiments cited by Harvard anthropologist Richard Wrangham, researchers found that there was a surge in testosterone levels among men who competed in a wide range of competitive activities from hand-to-hand fighting to chess matches. During the contest, testosterone levels reached their peak. But the most telling results appeared after the competitive activity was finished. There was a striking difference in the levels of this male hormone in winners versus losers. Among men who won, testosterone stayed high. Among the losers, it plummeted.

In other words, the good feelings that come from conquest are more than illusory. Men's glands actually pump out hormonal signals that say, "You're successful, you're important, you . . . won!" And, of course, there are numerous messages from colleagues and probably from members of the opposite sex that enhance and reinforce those good feelings of success. Men who win get promoted. They make more money. They attract lovely women. They achieve numerous forms of recognition that are denied those who lose.

Everyone wants to be a winner. No one wants to be a loser. Hence, men in particular as well as some women seem custom designed to obey the message that appears to have been stamped and imprinted on their very soul. They must obtain that moment of glory.

How Much Will You Pay?

How much will it cost us to get what we need to achieve? How much will we be forced to sacrifice? What stamina is required to make it to the top? How smart and quick do we have to be to make sure that no one takes advantage of us? How do we deny the impulses that could make us losers and acquire the conquering traits of winners?

I think most of us would admit unabashedly that we are looking for the right formula that will ensure success and insulate us from failure. Scan the best-seller lists and there will always be a title with advice and instructions on fighting back, maintaining dominance, and making sure you're never outfoxed. Enter any rung of any corporation and you will quickly grasp the underlying message: work your way up to a higher position, improve your salary, and reach the stratosphere of success where you can be a CEO who earns thirty-seven times the salary of an average worker. On a team, the goal is to be a leading scorer; in an academic setting, to be ranked number one in the class. The goal is to have the largest and most beautiful house on the block or the most expensive vehicle.

As for the all-American formulas, they are everywhere we turn. "Winning is a state of mind." "For successful people, the glass is half full, never half empty." "Never say never." "A winner never quits; a quitter never wins." And on. And on. And on.

But if winning is its own reward and if so many people are instinctively drawn to take pleasure from their own success, you might well ask why all this cheerleading and encouragement are necessary. Do we really enjoy winning so intensely that we happily accept the sacrifices that seem required to achieve success? Or are we actually engaged in something quite different—trying to tame anxiety, quell uncertainty, and escape the fear of failure? If winning brings us glory, then what's the flip side? What happens when we face the possibility of losing? And, to get to the most subtle but significant question of all, what is the personal meaning of winning and losing for each one of us?

These are more than academic questions. If you have performance addiction, losing is intolerable. Unfortunately, though, some people (again, by my observation, men more often than women) cannot even face the reality of their performance until they reach the point where they have won everything, and instead of feeling the rewards of victory, they feel that they have lost.

Finding the Remarkable in the Ordinary

We all have some sense of what it means to hit bottom. But what does it mean to hit the top and feel like you've hit bottom?

RAYMOND: MAKING A FORTUNE WITHOUT FEELING FORTUNATE

Raymond is sixty-one years old. He is the CEO of his own business, which he built from the ground up. It would be conceivable for him to make more money than he already does, but it is no longer an issue. Everything that money can buy is easily within reach.

I remember the first time I saw him twenty years ago. Patti, the youngest of his four children and his only daughter, had become my patient after an attempted suicide, and I felt it was essential to meet with her parents. Patti's mother, Pat, was available almost any time. But her father, Raymond, then forty-one, had a busy schedule and was constantly traveling. Four weeks passed before he could make an appointment to come in and talk about his daughter.

At the time, it seemed clear to me that Raymond had acute performance addiction. We had to talk about his health as well as his daughter's. Everyone in the family knew that Raymond's business came first, and Pat felt neglected. Patti, being the child who was closest to Pat, also identified with her, which certainly contributed to Patti's own depression. I recall thinking that Raymond's performance addiction was steering him toward disaster. As we concluded therapy, he talked about paying more attention to his wife and spending more time with his children. I expressed my concern that he was headed for a heart attack if he didn't make some changes, and he seemed to take my remarks seriously.

Now, twenty years later, Raymond is back. My fears about a heart attack were (fortunately) off the mark, but despite some efforts toward lifestyle changes, he has not really come to grips with his performance addiction. The issues remain. He continues to work long hours even though he doesn't need the extra income, and he is struggling to find ways to confront feelings that he has neglected. Those feelings came to the fore with the death of his wife, Pat.

She had advanced coronary heart disease. After her death, Raymond tells me, he fell apart. He couldn't sleep. He could hardly eat. After all the years of devoting himself to the business, he was haunted by what we had discussed twenty years ago. Back then, he had decided to spend more time with Pat and cultivate the relationship. It didn't happen. "I was afraid to be with my own wife," he tells me. "She worshipped me. And I was so consumed with growing the business that I missed all those years."

After Pat's death, Raymond dealt with his depression in a typical way. He took action. Within a few months, he met Judy, who was ten years younger. Not long afterward, they were married. Why this woman? And why so soon after Pat's death?

"Until I met Judy, I had no idea how to have fun. She loved to play. We were going all the time and the sex was great. It was an experience I'd never had before."

But this relationship is quickly coming to an end. At the time of their marriage, Raymond agreed to buy Judy a house in Hilton Head and put the home in her name. After the marriage, she pressured Raymond to set up trust funds for her two daughters. The relationship is deteriorating, and Judy seems "to want more and more. I think she is trying to rob me of every cent I ever earned." Raymond is not only depressed but ashamed: "I can't believe that a man with my business sense could be so fooled. I realize now I have no experience with women, with relationships—the things that really matter."

Not true, of course. His relationship with Pat spanned decades. But now he is asking himself what kind of relationship it was. "Pat just adored me. Everything was my way, and she let me spend hours upon hours trying everything I could to prove my worth. She worshipped me. I fell into a depression when she died, and when I met Judy, my spirit just came alive."

But why did Raymond have to prove his worth in his own eyes? Once he had a successful business, an adoring wife and children, what was that need to prove all about?

Raymond's father attended Princeton. So did his two brothers,

Geoffrey and Alan. From the very beginning, Raymond understood that he was supposed to go to an Ivy League school, but he was the only sibling who never made it.

His brother Geoffrey got his MBA and quickly became a multi-millionaire and CEO of a number of companies. His brother Alan went on to law school and is a partner in a major Atlanta firm. Raymond's father held up Geoffrey and Alan as role models, and chided Raymond for his lack of ambition. Raymond found Pat, who respected and even worshipped him unconditionally. To her it didn't matter that he was an academic failure and never made it to Princeton.

The devoted wife, the family, and the accumulation of wealth should have been consolation prizes, but they were never enough. No matter how hard Raymond worked and how much money he made, he never felt as if he measured up. Long ago, the image of loser was imprinted in his conscience, and even after thousands of days of dedicated work and sacrifice, Raymond has been unable to dispel the specter of his own failure. "Today I have all the money in the world," Raymond says, "and I still don't feel like I've made it. I am still striving for more and more."

One week Raymond missed a group session, and when he came to see me next, he explained why. He had attended the funeral of one of his father's best friends. I found this to be unusual. Raymond doesn't often miss appointments, and when he does, it's because something urgent has come up. Never before would he consider a funeral to be an urgent matter. Recognizing this, he reflects, "I am ashamed to admit it, but I never went to funerals or wakes. I thought I couldn't afford to miss work. I always had Pat, who would go in my place."

But Pat's death inspired an outpouring of sympathy and concern that made a strong impression. "I was showered with affection. People called, they sent food, they were so generous. Of course, I knew it was for Pat and not for me."

As Raymond experienced depression, fell madly in love again, remarried, and is now struggling in a painful and loveless marriage, he feels as if something has changed in him. "I have learned in the last year that the ordinary things people do are the exceptional things," he says. "Going to a wake, bringing food to the home of the deceased, sending a card, attending a wedding, calling a friend—all these things that I considered ordinary, below me. . . . How foolish was I?"

From Patti, the daughter who once attempted suicide, Raymond has also learned something quite "ordinary"—that it is possible to relax and enjoy life without pursuing status as ardently as he had done in his own life. Patti is not an achiever, at least not in Raymond's old terms, but she is a good person and has a lot of fun in her life.

Ironically enough, some of the other ordinary things he neglected were in his own self-interest, even though he thought he never had time for them. He now exercises regularly. He has started to pay attention to his eating habits. Raymond is taking better care of himself.

But what about the old battles—the failure to get in to Princeton, the lack of ambition that so irked his father, and Raymond's competition with the smart, rich brothers who could do no wrong? Somehow, the role models and the measures of status have not stood the test of time. "I idealized my brothers all my life," says Raymond. "Now I realize they are both miserable." Geoffrey is obese. He has never married and has no friends. Alan is married to an alcoholic who refuses treatment and is the father of two adult children who are completely estranged from him.

Raymond says, "I've been thinking that I had blinders on all my life. I thought I could buy love. Now I realize that all the accomplishments in the world won't buy love."

He acknowledges that it's something he knew all along. But intellectual understanding and emotional drives are separate. As long as he had blinders on, Raymond could make himself believe that life's rewards were almost within reach. All he had to do was strive more, work harder, and prove himself. But his losses rather than his victories have brought him within range of things that really matter to him—the ordinary things to which he never assigned any worth. Raymond has come to the realization that he will never be loved for what he does, only for who he is. "I think I finally get it," he says.

Who Are Your Heroes?

Was Raymond's idealization of his brothers an expression of envy or healthy competitiveness? Male heroes, it seems to me, are objects of admiration and resentment. But the need for icons is transparent. It's no coincidence that sports figures are so commonly discussed, praised, and admired almost to the point of reverence by men who literally project themselves onto the performance of their heroes. (Nor is it a coincidence that the larger-than-life public personae of these figures is so often accompanied by a personal inability to deal with fame, wealth, and adulation.) So many of us want heroes who are better than ourselves, and the greater their feats, the more we want to respect them.

Measuring ourselves against figures who seem to be giants, it is easy to acknowledge the differences between "them" and "us." It stands to reason that public figures do not share their private insecurities with the world at large. But what happens when those who are close to us hide their humanness from us? What if they are just as remotely positioned and misunderstood as the professional ballplayer who pitches a shutout or the quarterback with a record-setting season?

We need heroes who are human, and if we don't get a glimpse of their humanness, I believe the search for glory can become never-ending. One thing is certain, however. We ourselves can never become icons. No matter what we do, we are bound to the thoughts, emotions, doubts, yearnings, and losses that make us vulnerable. As Raymond discovered, it is the ordinary things that make us exceptional. The rest is a matter of how we are perceived.

This is the real trouble with the kind of ambition that feeds performance addiction. Not the rivalry that we have with others—because, indeed, there are rewards to be found in intense competition. Certainly not respect or admiration—for we have every reason to hold some people in high esteem. Not even the wish to be successful—because it is gratifying to have a feeling of accomplishment. No, the danger lies in the expectation that competition, accomplishment, and success will nurture affection, appreciation, and love. All the components that give us those nurturing rewards—the parts of us that we describe as soul or character—are quite apart from the competitive, status-conscious need for approbation, recognition, and wealth. Just as love is no guarantee of success in our society, success is no guarantee of affection.

When someone has performance addiction, however, the two goals are confused. Just as the alcoholic can make himself believe that he loves and is loved by everyone, someone with performance addiction can temporarily sustain the illusion that intellectual, financial, social, or political success can fuel a bonfire of vanity that will burn away the need for love and respect. It is only when the losses begin to accumulate as they did with Raymond that the blinders fall away.

The Stress of Performance Addiction

Men with performance addiction are capable of an extraordinary amount of denial. In some high-stress, traumatic circumstances, denial is a magnificent survival mechanism. But it is definitely a mechanism, and in day-to-day life, it doesn't serve us well.

The denial of pain, for instance. What better way to become a respected athlete? "Play through the pain" is the working motto, whether you're a football player, a speed swimmer, or a runner. In the world of intense competition, the best thing you can do is ignore pain. This paradigm—to suck it in, push yourself to the limits, and tough it out—is the essence of military as well as physical training. In these arenas, the paradigm works.

But what about transferring the virtues of stamina and endurance to other kinds of professional training? To become a medical doctor, you must endure round-the-clock rotations. In law school or any other intensely competitive field of professional training, stamina is as highly valued as creativity. As women have moved into these traditionally male-dominated bastions of competition, they have been forced to accept the norms. The only way to be successful at these endeavors is to meet the tests. And the tests are not solely measures of accomplishment, skill, and performance. They are also measures of discipline, sacrifice, denial of personal feelings, and stoicism.

There are ample rewards for those who pass the endurance tests and also meet performance measures. Compare the average salaries of medical doctors, lawyers, and business school graduates to those who drop out or fail. Compare the highly successful professional athlete to the athlete who doesn't make the cut. Compare the businessperson who can endure endless travel and meetings and get by on a few hours of sleep to the one who guards personal time and is cautious about overcommitment. Is there any question about who the "winners" are or how they do it? Clearly, as we recognize and reward it, success requires other qualities, as well. It takes stamina and persistence to make it as a professional.

But now I'm hearing the uneasiness of men whose whole careers have been built on carefully constructed, magnificently maintained assumptions about the sacrifices they need to make and the pain they need to ignore in order to be successful. Yes, their assumptions were correct. They paid the price and they have achieved success as they understood it. But now what?

Unfortunately, the success that has been achieved by means of denial cannot be maintained by the same means. It's not just the terms of success that have changed. It's the word itself. What does *success* mean when it ceases to have meaning?

Anger and Frustration

Many men are willing to risk everything to avoid their deep fear of failing. Unfortunately, they have not learned how to love or be loved in any other way but through successful performance. Their drive to win is a mask that hides their tremendous anxieties about being imperfect.

Tony: Building a Business, Losing a Father

Nearly every man in our performance addiction group identifies with Tony, though he did not come from an Ivy League background or climb the ladder of success through college and graduate school. His background is blue collar. But his performance addiction is the same as many other men and women who have reached the top in their chosen career or profession.

From the very beginning, Tony seemed destined to take over his father's successful construction business. Initially he defied his parents' wishes by getting an associate degree at a community college, though his father insisted that it wasn't necessary. Punitive, hard-driving, and a stickler for details, Tony's father rode him hard. When Tony finally joined the business, tempers flared, and eventually there was a blowout between father and son. For eighteen months, Tony and his father were not on speaking terms. Then his father had a stroke and died.

Tony was devastated. He went to the funeral, but his mother and brothers shunned him. Though Tony took over the business after his father's death, the family ties were broken. Meanwhile, the construction company has flourished. When Tony first came to see me, the company was having its best year ever. But the better things went, the worse Tony felt. He couldn't understand it.

At one point, Tony had to be out of the office for two days because he had been having heart trouble and needed tests. When he came back, he lost his temper at one of the foremen and launched a blistering attack. The foreman showed him the assignment board listing all the jobs. The crews were actually ahead of schedule.

The truth is starting to sink in. Tony is in a position that should be enviable. The business can run itself. He doesn't even need to be there. He now realizes that even if he showed up only one or two days a week, everything could move ahead without him. Why the anger? Why the sinking feeling?

Tony's wife is very familiar with her husband's anger. She calls it his trigger reaction. He anticipates that something will go wrong, and his anger grows. Tony explains, "I absolutely know that something is not going to happen in the way I need it to and the dam bursts!" But before he reaches the trigger point, there are actually stages: the growing sense of failure and the perception that "we are not going to succeed." And, finally, the explosion.

Who can calm him down? His mentor is gone. The business has succeeded but not Tony. He hasn't forgiven himself or been forgiven. Tears come to his eyes when I ask him about his father.

Recently Tony's company won a national award and was featured in a number of newspapers. When Tony was interviewed, the reporter asked him about the beginning of the business. Uneasily at first, then with growing assurance, Tony answered the reporter's questions about how he got started in construction. Tony found he took pride in talking about the company and how his father had started it. Finally it dawned on him: "I was trying to say, 'Dad, I forgive you. I love you. I am publicly acknowledging it wasn't all bad between us.'"

Shortly afterward, Tony prepared to meet with his mother. He went with a strong resolution to tolerate her criticism and remain focused on reestablishing the relationship. She did talk about her disappointment in him. But as he left, he was able to say, "Mom, I love you." She replied, "I love you, too." Her words were almost inaudible. But as she spoke, Tony realized he could not ever remember her saying those words to him or anyone else.

In group, when Tony describes how difficult it is for him to let go of his work, others nod in recognition. "I know I push myself to produce to gain love and respect," one man responded recently. "The problem is, I don't know how to experience love any other way. I think I may be incapable of loving anyone except my children."

The Religion of Perfection

After many years of personal investment, work becomes more like a religion than a vocation. And what are the principles that under-lie any religion? There is the mythology of reward and punish-ment—that we will be rewarded in spiritual or material ways for doing right and will be punished for doing wrong. From that clear dichotomy comes the hierarchy of perfectibility. In the religion of perfection, we are always somewhere on the ladder that leads toward improvement but always fearful that backsliding will plunge us into the abyss. The risks of giving up work are as serious as those associated with giving up religion. Without faith, where will we end up? Without a hierarchy of getting better in every way, what will happen to us?

Tony feels he needs to "find something else." But what is that something else? He has always lived by performance measures. Unless he uses those measurements to evaluate himself and the people around him, how will he know whether he is pursuing something that has value and worth?

This will not be an easy search for Tony, and it's far from over. He needs to deal with his own fear of letting go, and he will have to discover the emotions that he has successfully denied for many years—feelings associated with the loss of his father and, through estrangement, his entire family. His religion of perfection has sus-tained his efforts, but as the gap has widened between successful performance and feelings of success, he has become increasingly nervous, restless, and plagued by stress. Inevitably, his health has been affected and the early warning signs of heart disease cannot be ignored.

But as Tony talks to others in the group and realizes he is not as isolated as he once thought, a calmness emerges. On a recent Father's Day, Tony learned that his eldest son was calling around to other members of the family to find out what he should get his dad. The son, like his father, is a very busy man. He usually buys a gift and drops it off. This year, Tony told every family member, "When Chuck calls to ask what I want, have him call me directly." Finally his son did just that. "I only want one thing from you," Tony told him. "It's the one thing my father could never give me. I want us to spend time together."

Finding Your Dimmer Switch

We all need a dimmer switch, but many performance addicts simply can't find it. They're either on or off. There's no midrange. The "on" state is complete commitment, fourteen-hour workdays, never settle for second best, and go for the goal. The "off" is collapse, "I don't know what to do with myself," and "I'm failing."

Why do we set performance expectations so high that we cannot possibly sustain the energy needed to meet those expectations? At what point does the religion of perfection become so all-encompassing that one little slip represents a fall from grace?

With practice, it's possible to exercise greater control over your own dimmer switch so that you don't have to be either "on" or "off." Your goal is to be able to reach the previously mentioned state of calm energy described by Robert Thayer. Though Thayer deals largely with regulating mood with food and exercise, many of his observations are relevant to performance addiction:

> Since people differ in exactly when and under what conditions these mood shifts occur, . . . effective management requires sharpening awareness of moods, and this is where self-study becomes extremely valuable. It is essential to become familiar with the full range of your variations in energy and tension, not just the highest and lowest levels. In other words, it is important to recognize subtle variations in your moods.

This recognition of basic mood changes requires practice. When people are under stress it is easy to overlook mild tense tiredness—the kind of mood that breaks down resolve and inevitably leads to broken diets and skipped exercise. While extreme tension is recognized by most, mild tension becomes second nature to the person who works long hours under constant deadlines. . . . The effects of this almost undetectable state eventually emerge. . . . But the underlying mood causes often go unnoticed.

Being able to acknowledge your underlying moods is essential if you want to overcome performance addiction. But apart from the self-recognition of mood variations, I believe there is another extremely powerful force that can help control the dimmer switch. That force is empathy.

Empathic Immersion

Performance addicts tend to spend an inordinate amount of time thinking about how to improve themselves, how to reach the next level of excellence. They don't realize there is a way out of this internal prison, a mental vacation that is always within reach: the capacity for empathy. To restore ourselves, we need to lose ourselves in another person's experience.

PAUL: DISCOVERING HE DOESN'T FLY ALONE

Paul was a star soccer player and superb student in high school, and he graduated from an Ivy League college. Today he is a successful corporate executive who logs in thousands of miles of travel every year. But his performance anxiety goes into high gear, particularly on long trips when he faces high-pressure meetings. Paul is prone to alcohol abuse and addicted to chewing tobacco. He usually gets through long plane flights by drinking and chewing, and trying to blot out everything around him.

This time he wants it to be different. The challenge is how to get to the West Coast without drinking and chewing the whole way. Self-discipline? Self-control?

For someone who is constantly under pressure, additional rules and advice are hardly the answer. Instead, we talk about how he seems to relax whenever he gets involved in talking to another person. I've noticed in group sessions that his self-consciousness seems to vanish when he allows himself to be absorbed in another person's world.

"Why don't you try something new on this trip?" I suggest. "Start a conversation with the person sitting next to you. Ask some open-ended questions. Use empathy. You never know—it could give you a mental vacation from your own worries."

Two weeks later, during a group session after Paul has returned from his trip, I ask him how it went. He starts to tell me about it, then stops, choking up. He tries to recover. This is hard.

Paul followed my suggestion. Instead of opening his laptop immediately, he started to make small talk with the woman next to him. At one point he took a risk and mentioned that he was anxious about the upcoming meetings, and she replied by saying she was also anxious. He inquired, and she told him this was her first week back to work after a long absence. Her son, the valedictorian of his high school class and in college on a track scholarship, was found dead in his room. She learned that he was a cocaine user, and his death was an apparent suicide.

Paul, who seldom cries, could barely speak as he tried to relate the rest of the experience. He said he was mesmerized as he listened to this brokenhearted stranger. Paul went on to relate how the woman described her son's funeral. Two uncles convinced the boy's younger brother to compete in his high school cross-country meet that afternoon. They believed his brother would have wanted his sibling to run. Even though he did not possess his older brother's ability, the boy ran his best time ever. As he entered the stadium, every one of his competitors let him pass as they cheered for him in honor of his brother. He could not have beaten them even on his best day.

Paul was sobbing at this point, and every member of the group had tears in their eyes. He said he never once thought of chewing or drinking during the flight.

"I wonder why this story affected me so much," he asked. I suggested that maybe the young man who committed suicide had, like Paul, become addicted to succeeding. Maybe performance became everything, and he lost his perspective as to what really brings a person love and respect.

As he talked about this experience, Paul's expression changed. There was a newly detectable calmness. Paul had come face-to-face with his own imperfections and learned that empathic interactions naturally change our neurochemistry.

Instead of trying to make his insecurities disappear through alcohol and nicotine, he found that empathic immersion gave him a way to accept those insecurities and deal with them. By revealing his emotions and imperfections, he gained a stronger sense of self and a far greater acceptance of his own humanness. Mutual empathy not only gave him what he had been looking for through performance but also produced a calmness he desperately needed.

What You Can Do about Performance Addiction

If you answered yes to any of the questions at the beginning of this chapter, I urge you to think creatively about your personal attitudes toward your work, your expectations about what you hope to achieve, and the rewards you feel you deserve. These writing assignments will help you.

Does your work title lack the prestige you really desire?

WRITING ASSIGNMENT: Describe your fantasy of the ideal job, including title and financial package. As you think about that ideal, try to decide what's most attractive about it: the work itself or the prestige associated with it? Is your drive to be in that position based on your qualifications, or is it based on an attempt to make yourself "whole" emotionally? Describe the factors that matter the most to you.

Do you find yourself constantly calculating how much money you are making?

WRITING ASSIGNMENT: Write a description of the ways your life would be enhanced if your home were more luxurious, your car more expensive, or your portfolio larger. Ask your partner or spouse if he or she agrees.

Describe how you feel when friends or associates buy things that you cannot afford. What emotions does their capability engender in you? What do you assume their wealth means about them? About you?

Finally, describe financial goals that are realistic and healthy for you to pursue. As you think about these objectives, try to distinguish between what you really need to enhance your lifestyle. (That's not the same as wishing for money that will prove you're a winner or exceed the wealth of a rival.) Evaluate whether you have already achieved those realistic and healthy financial goals or what you will have to do to reach them.

Are you easily impressed by another person's credentials?

WRITING ASSIGNMENT: List any person with whom you would like to change places. Include any celebrities or athletes, and describe the aspects of their lifestyle that you wish for the most. Do you feel that you deserve what they have and feel cheated because you don't have it?

Describe exactly what exists in their life that is missing in yours. Explain how those missing ingredients would permanently alter your life if you could obtain them.

Do you tend to idealize those who have power, regardless of their character?

WRITING ASSIGNMENT: List the people you know who clearly lead joyous lives. What ingredients have led to their happiness? What is their perspective on life? How does their perspective compare to yours?

Think about how driven you are to gain recognition and admiration in your work. Compare that to how devoted you are to gain recognition and admiration from your family and friends. Describe the part of your life that attracts the greatest portion of your attention. If there are things you would like to do to balance the equation, list some specific steps.

9

Meaning and Joy

1. Do you experience joy only when you are impressing others with your wit and charm?

2. Do you seldom find meaning in solitary activities?

3. Do you find meaning in the outcomes of situations but seldom in the process?

PERFORMANCE ADDICTION IS A THIEF of simple pleasures. For someone who enjoys sports, the demand to improve performance steals joy from the exercise. A talented musician can't bask in the pleasure of his own gifts or even get gratification from listening and playing because he is fraught with anxiety about making a single mistake. For someone who becomes totally focused on success, moments are measured in terms of progress and relationships are scrutinized to calibrate their worth. Taken to the extreme, these pressures are relentless.

AARON: STAGE FRIGHT BEFORE THE BASEBALL GAME

Aaron volunteered to pitch at the parent-faculty softball tournament for the benefit of his daughter's private school.

He knew he wasn't a great softball player, but what did he have to lose? He enjoyed softball, and it was all for a good cause. His daughter and her friends would be there cheering. Aaron was psyched.

The night before the tournament, he got sick. By morning, he felt as if he could barely walk, much less pitch several innings in front of a crowd. He called in sick, much to the disappointment of his daughter. He wasn't faking it, of course. He really felt rotten.

But the whole episode reminded him of something, which came back to him later. As a football player in high school, he had convinced himself that he was a lousy player and he would vomit before each game. Here he was, twenty years later, doing it again. But why? What made the stakes so high?

Aaron had the same clenching fear he'd had in college that he was going to lose, look ridiculous, and let people down. What should have been a day of enjoyment for him became a struggle with self-will and self-image. His daughter had no idea what was going on. She was sorry he got sick and disappointed that he was not among the parents who showed up that day. She did not know that the prospect of an enjoyable game turned into the threat of an excruciating trial for her father.

Discovering What Really Matters

As Aaron's experience shows, the deprivation of joy can be insidious. We actually lose the ability to accept the bonuses that are placed right in front of us. After all, for a performance addict, what could be more gratuitous and therefore more suspect than to be given a reward without asking, working, or striving for it? When rewards are free, can we trust them? Are they real? And if they are, why didn't someone tell us earlier? Why work so hard for accomplishment and acceptance if the simple joys can be had for nothing?

If you have performance addiction, meaning should come through hard work, not through good fortune. Such serendipity is an insult to the system and a defiance of the religion. As contradictory as it may seem, it's extremely difficult to give up a system of beliefs that's so insistent in its demands and so dogmatic in its dictates. Like any free offer, unearned joy is likely to be greeted with skepticism, suspicion, and even hostility.

Performance addiction is rarely given up without a struggle. When you stumble across moments of intense reward without having earned them, you may feel that your life as you knew it has lost its meaning. If performance doesn't matter, what does? This was the question that Jordan had to face.

JORDAN: UNSHACKLING FROM THE WORK ETHIC

Jordan never graduated from college, yet he is a well-paid manager in one of the leading security firms in Boston. His manner is quiet and reserved, and some members of the group have encouraged him to talk more. They can feel him struggling with his own reticence, but from his few contributions they can tell that he is intelligent, well meaning, and sensitive. The fact that he has come so far in his career without a college degree speaks for itself. He is ambitious and hardworking, though in performance evaluations his supervisors have said they would like him to be more assertive. He has quiet strength, and I would guess that in a professional setting people tend to have great confidence in him.

That confidence, however, is not shared by Jordan himself. Growing up, he was influenced by his mother, who had great ambitions for him. (His dad, however, was an absent father.) No matter what he did, Jordan felt as if he constantly disappointed his mother. His first marriage to a demanding and disapproving woman mirrored his relationship to his mother, and it was his ex-wife who eventually ended the marriage, largely because he never fulfilled her expectations. Now remarried, he has a ten-year-old daughter, Amy, from his first marriage. Whenever Amy comes to visit for the weekend, Jordan has noticed that she always leaves something behind. Invariably, he has to stop off at his ex's house on Monday to return a pair of shoes or a notebook.

For a number of years, Jordan has been in steady recovery from alcohol addiction. The progress is significant. He is now on better terms with his present wife. He is less judgmental about himself, his career path, and his measurements of success.

In the past, Jordan not only took his mother's criticism deeply to heart but he also accepted the way she often compared him to his sister, who went to college, graduate school, and is now a highly regarded sociologist with tenure at a large university. Jordan's mother always called to let him know when his sister would be on a TV talk show, then phoned afterward to make sure he had watched the show. After four or five minutes of listening to his mother's exclamations of wonder—"She's so confident! Isn't it amazing how poised she is?"—Jordan would be boiling with unexpressed rage. He never told his mother what he actually thought of his sister's pontifications. "Dull, didactic, and loony" was how he described them to me.

As irritated as he was by his mother's excessive worship of his sibling, Jordan got along perfectly well with his sister. But he refused to be honest with his mother. Sarcastic, yes. Silent and removed, as necessary. Brusque and defensive, at times. When his mother launched into a lecture about everything Jordan should be doing, he never showed anger. That wasn't his style. But the rage had to go somewhere, so he turned it on himself.

The cycle of blame went something like this: "I've failed in the past because I didn't work hard enough. I didn't put enough into it. I can't change that, but I can be more disciplined. I can be careful I don't make the same mistakes again. I can work harder. I'll never succeed, but at least I will have done everything I could, so no one can say I didn't try my best."

At the same time, there was the angry rebel. Part of Jordan remained defiant, even destructive: "If I'm a failure, then I'll go ahead and prove it. I'll screw things up so badly, everyone will give up on me and leave me alone."

When the war of self-blame was at its peak, the alcohol helped. At least it dulled the rage. And when Jordan drank enough, he proved to himself that the part about failure was certainly accurate. What better way to display total incapacitation?

But now Jordan had set himself to the new task of exploring his rage, sharing his insecurities, and talking with some honesty about his inner life. For the recovering alcoholic—the person who could no longer accept the easy definition of himself as a failure—the recovery process had turned into a search for meaning. If he gave up the struggle he had always accepted as important and necessary—to work harder, compensate for past mistakes, achieve a measure of respectability and prestige, and prove his self-worth in some small way—then what was left? What new avenues was he supposed to pursue? How could he claim his own territory and find a new area of acceptability?

It was truly a search for meaning. Jordan struggled with the rage, needing a way to express it but fearing that he would hurt others. He struggled with the work ethic, understanding that no career advancement would ever be enough, yet terrified that if he gave in to his feelings of laziness and disenchantment, he would turn into a slacker. He struggled with his mother, wanting to defy her illusions about his ever-bright potential, yet afraid of wounding her.

Not surprisingly, in the grip of these warring forces, Jordan sometimes appeared dazed. In group meetings, he became removed and distracted, as if he couldn't quite focus or find his place. On one of these occasions, someone asked him what he was thinking about and what was happening in his life.

"Oh, nothing," was his first response. His marriage was the same; so was his job. Then someone asked about his daughter. Others smiled along with Jordan as he told the group how Amy was always leaving something at his house when she stayed over.

"The other night," he went on, "I had to return her sweater and running shoes." That meant driving over to his ex's house, but she wasn't home. "My daughter answered the door. She was all smiles. I handed over her things, and then I said to her, 'I know why you forget things all the time.' She looked at me like she expected a lecture about responsibilities. I said, 'It's because you want a hug from your dear old dad!' She gave me a big smile, and to make a long story short, I got my hug."

Tears filled his eyes as he told us. Afterward, Jordan expressed amazement that he had stumbled on these feelings about his daughter. Unquestionably, he had always cared about her, been happy when he was with her, and enjoyed watching her grow up. But that had been easy. He simply loved her. There were no demands, expectations, or measurements. Being a father was just something that you were, not something that you did.

Without even paying attention, he had relegated that part of his life to a position of secondary importance. True to the religion of performance addiction, Jordan had always assumed that meaningful accomplishments required work, sacrifice, and dedication. But getting a hug from his daughter—where was the challenge in that? Yet that reward felt better than everything he had struggled so purposefully to achieve.

It was certainly characteristic that Jordan was disappointed in himself because he hadn't been able to discover this simple truth on his own. It required the observation of someone else in the group to help him realize that "being alone, in your own mind, led you to feel empty in the first place. When you asked your daughter for a hug, you got one."

Jordan's struggle to find meaning could be successful only when he gave up the struggle. Meaning came through genuine involvement and genuine expression, not by pursuing goals that were based on a faulty mirroring of who Jordan was supposed to be or what he was supposed to do. He had lived with myths about the meaningful rewards that performance would provide. He had hammered himself with reminders that he was never good enough and that he couldn't measure up. All the while, he had been neglecting a truer aspect of his own character that defied measurement. The realization of meaning and the true feeling of joy came from the simple human impulse to embrace his daughter, not from the complex and exhausting exercise of jumping through hoops.

SELF-EVALUATION:
YOUR SEARCH FOR TRUE JOY

Do you lead a joyful existence? If not, where have you misled yourself and for what reasons? The following quiz will help you learn more about these issues. Answer each question as quickly as possible. Most of the questions require one-word answers.

1. How often do you laugh heartily?
2. Do you need to be drinking or taking drugs to do so?
3. Do friends and associates consider you to have a good sense of humor in sober situations?
4. Do you find yourself trying to be funny to win approval?
5. Do you use your wit in a condescending manner?
6. Do you use your wit in a self-deprecating manner?
7. Do you use humor to avoid intimate situations?
8. How often does your humor flow from a state of being totally comfortable with people?
9. How often is your humor driven by your anxiety?
10. Do you know what if feels like to be totally calm?
11. Is your life course other directed? (Other directed means that your major life choices are determined by your need

to please others, rather than being based on your own desires—for example, if you went to business school because your father told you it was the way to make money, or if you married a lawyer because your mother said lawyers make great providers.)

12. Have the major choices in your life been heavily influenced by what you believe are others' expectations?

13. If you have children:

> Do you find it tedious to spend considerable time with them?

> When you're with them, do you often think about how you could be getting so much done if you didn't have to take care of them?

> Do you feel they have little to contribute until they are able to converse intelligently?

14. Do you derive peace of mind from being at the ocean or in the mountains?

15. Do you find yourself frustrated on a weekend away because you just can't unwind and enjoy nature?

16. How often do you have flow state experiences (i.e., through exercise, expressing love, listening to music, listening to the ocean)?

17. How balanced is your typical week? Do you spend a reasonable amount of time alone, with family, friends, working, playing?

18. What important aspect of your life gets the least amount of your time?

19. What aspect gets most of your time?

20. Are you satisfied with this equation?

21. What would an inner-directed person want to change if he or she were living your life?

When you have answered all the questions, take a moment to review your answers. Ask yourself how many are related to performance addiction. Can you identify the times that have brought you true joy unrelated to the way you are perceived by others or the rewards you feel you have to earn? Ask yourself how you can redirect your life so that meaning and joy are maximized.

Are You Making a Living or Having a Life?

In *The Future of Success: Working and Living in the New Economy,* former secretary of labor Robert B. Reich puts the dilemma of Jordan's search for meaning into a socioeconomic context. I suspect that Reich's observations—based on his experience in government, academia, and business—resonate with many of us.

"Most Americans," reflects Reich, "seem genuinely to be seeking more balanced lives. The problem is that balance between making a living and making a life is becoming harder to pull off because the logic of the new economy dictates that more attention be paid to work and less to personal life."

Jordan and everyone else in this country are faced with many dilemmas when it comes to making choices about work and family. As Reich outlines with all the statistical resources at his command, the people who have the top positions in their professions and are the uppermost salary earners also spend the most time at work. We may wish to spend more hours with our children or families or doing community work, but how can we steal the time? Everyone's work environment has become more competitive and precarious. Unless you're enjoying tenure at a well-endowed university or drifting under the canopy of a golden parachute, your job may actually be in jeopardy. This is the new reality of the workplace.

Jordan regrets that he didn't spend more time with his daughter in her earlier years, but the decisions he made about working hard and developing his career were solid, understandable, and necessary. As Reich points out, personal choices about how hard to work "are not really personal choices at all because the advantages of working harder for pay and the disadvantages of not doing so, as well as the benefits and the costs of living in one community or another, are larger today than they used to be, and larger in America than in many other countries."

Like many Americans who have gone through divorce, Jordan's financial and professional demands took an exacting toll on his time. The fact that he had come to a crossroads where his relationship with his daughter was becoming more important and his career less so did not in any way reflect badly on the choices he had made earlier. These are choices we all make, and the current conditions of competitiveness, mobility, and uncertainty in American society do not make those choices any easier.

But the balance that we achieve in our lives has more to do with perspective and values than with allocation of hours to work, family, and recreation. A telling statistic cited by Reich is that "American parents now spend on average twenty-two fewer hours each week with their children than did parents thirty years ago." Many demographic facts are implicit in those statistics—that there are more single-parent families, more two-earner families, and fewer children—but the baseline fact is that we are spending less time with our children.

Jordan cannot reverse that trend on his own. None of us can. But the choices that we make about how to spend our time are much more difficult if we are driven by the unacknowledged and subconscious demands of performance addiction. Jordan has realized that no amount of professional achievement can bring him joy. But just because he has reached this understanding, it does not mean he will give up his job (obviously) or even cut back on his work hours to spend more time with his daughter. Knowing about his addiction, however, Jordan can now exercise choices with greater awareness. His relationship with his daughter can bring him rewards that he could not possibly achieve through fierce, assiduous, and dedicated application of the work ethic. He may or may not become the regional manager or even come close. But whatever happens, he can still ask for a hug from his daughter and get it. The question is: Will he be able to hold on to his understanding of just how valuable that is?

Sounds simple. But when you have performance addiction, nothing is simple. When your mind is set on higher achievements, what's immediate, unearned, and free for the asking somehow seems too easy.

Escape Routes

While performance addiction has a demonstrable impact on relationships, this ingenious foe can steal simple joys and pleasures in many other ways, as well. "Here's the strange thing," says Reich. "The richer you are, the more likely it is that you are putting in long and harried hours at work, even obsessing about it when you're not doing it. A frenzied work life may or may not make you better off, but being better off definitely seems to carry with it more frenzy."

Many of us really can't get any time off from the frenzy. Work follows us into the weekend. It pursues us on vacations. We have many ways to stay in touch through computers, cell phones, electronic organizers, and beepers, and even when we're not using them, we're aware of being on call and available. In fact, in a competitive environment, it seems necessary to stay available so that we're not seen as ignoring our responsibilities or forfeiting opportunities. Don't you need to be reachable if there are key decisions to be made? How would you feel if a once-in-a-lifetime opportunity slipped away because someone couldn't get in touch with you by e-mail or phone?

But beyond these internal issues that stir anxiety and make you feel guilty about escaping, there may be other forces as well that deprive you of free time. As time off becomes shorter and dearer, you may feel as if every moment needs to be well spent. For performance addicts, vacation itself is a test of the ability to really use time well.

KEVIN: A TEST OF WILL

Kevin has planned a truly wonderful getaway that perfectly suits his temperament, feeds his wanderlust, and indulges one of his greatest pleasures. A young engineer with a high-tech company, Kevin has a passion for classic British sports cars. He owns a 1963 Jaguar convertible that he has tinkered with for years. Anticipating a classic car rally in Virginia, he has the car in the shop getting a final tune-up in preparation for the thousand-mile trip. It is truly the ultimate vacation—a long, enjoyable road trip and the chance to hang out with other classic car enthusiasts for a week.

But as the countdown continues, Kevin's anticipation seems to be turning to agitation. The mechanic who is working on the car has had some delays. Kevin feels let down. The car will be ready on Friday but only just in time, and Kevin will hardly have a chance to test-drive it. Meanwhile, a friend who is headed for the same rally in an early-model roadster has decided that it's not safe to drive that far. There are too many chances of a breakdown or accident. Kevin's friend is going to have his car transported to Virginia instead. As the day of departure draws near, Kevin starts referring to his upcoming vacation as "the challenge."

"Are you thinking that maybe your friend is right?" I asked. "Maybe it's not safe to drive all that way?"

Yes, Kevin has started to reevaluate the situation. Maybe it really is better to transport the car, but that poses a dilemma. He's already told lots of people that he plans to drive. How can he "chicken out" now? He talks about how embarrassing it would be to admit to his friends and his fellow engineers at work that he might not be able to handle any problems that might arise.

We go on to examine the concept of being chicken. Why wouldn't it be okay to say that the car had been late leaving the shop? Based on Kevin's own evaluation of the situation and the mechanic's advice, it seems reasonable that he needs to test the car before making a long trip. Surely his friends would regard this decision as displaying wisdom, not a sign that he had lost his nerve.

Kevin reflected for a moment. "Am I still trying to prove my worth? Is it that all over again?"

At that moment, we both knew what he was asking. With his long-anticipated vacation not even started yet, already the pleasure was being drained away by forces that felt like they were beyond his control. Throughout the early stages of preparation, Kevin had enjoyed the absolute certainty that everything would be perfect. The car would be in mint condition. It would leave the shop right on schedule precisely tuned and prepped for the long trip. Kevin would demonstrate that he was capable of impeccable planning and masterly execution. And now this! The danger of mechanical problems, the risk that he might not finish the trip or might arrive late, and the embarrassment of confessing to friends and colleagues that he hadn't be able to make it.

We talked further, drifting back to the scene of the crime. There was Kevin's father coming home from work and bragging to his son, his wife, and anyone who would listen about the life insurance policies he had sold that day. More policies than anyone else and better deals, too. In fact, one year when two salesmen had been let go, Kevin's father had stepped in and sold more life insurance than the other two salesmen combined. His father could do anything. "He was always so certain. He always had an answer," Kevin recalled. "The irony is, he usually was right."

Growing up in the shadow of a man like that, when Kevin learned that there was really only one path to certainty. If he started a project, he felt as if it needed to come out exactly as he predicted. If he made plans, they had to be executed with precision. It was Kevin's role to fix things, make them work, and prove that he had the answers.

So we talked about pathological certainty—that is, the absolute conviction that some people really do have a monopoly on the right answers. For the person with pathological certainty, outcomes should be a forgone conclusion. The plan must be followed. Deviation is a sign of weakness. As Kevin so succinctly put it, if you show uncertainty, you're chickening out.

His father had never chickened out. How could Kevin? Fortunately, he did. He put the Jaguar on a truck and headed south. The trip was not at all what he had anticipated, but he called it "the best vacation of my life." The freedom was not only a new discovery but absolutely exhilarating.

Stumbling on Joy

Can you recognize joy when it comes your way? Can you permit yourself to accept it? When you have been trained from birth to see yourself in terms of accomplishments, what can be said about the self that stands without accomplishment? What about good things that just happen? For great joy and happiness and true feelings of self-worth and fulfillment, aren't you really supposed to expend a great deal of energy? Don't you have to do the right thing at the right time in order to fulfill your potential? Some performance addicts know from experience that what starts out being a simple pleasure will end up being a teeth-clenching test of grit, will, and determination.

CHARLES: FINDING HIS GAME

Charles is in his forties and loves to play tennis. But despite his affection for the game, he knows he can enjoy it only under certain conditions. Charles understands what will happen if he hangs out at the club and starts to compete. He'll have to win. To win, he'll have to improve his game. To improve his game, he'll have to analyze what he's doing, which means finding fault with his current performance, practicing and striving to make it better, and working harder until the joy is gone. The warm-ups, games, matches, and tournaments will all turn into one grand measure of who

Charles is, how good he is, and how dedicated he is. Each stroke will become a test of whether he can improve himself.

To prevent the full measure of his performance addiction from kicking in and depriving him of this modest but important pleasure, Charles only plays with his wife and never at the club. Fortunately, he doesn't feel like he has to beat his wife at every game. These games with his wife are a gift—a little break from the performance measures that he imposes on other aspects of his life.

In the meantime, Charles has made another important discovery about himself and his own game. He is delighted when his wife hits a great passing shot. He loves a good volley, regardless of who wins it. When his wife delivers a fast serve, whether or not Charles gets to it in time, his internal response is "Wow!"

Telling me about this, Charles seems almost rueful. Is he turning into some kind of Pollyanna? But I think I get it. I think he has permitted himself to escape the monologue of performance addiction and enter the dialogue that lies at the center of joyful experience. This dialogue frees him from self-consciousness, self-judgment, and even self-destruction.

I am reminded of a quote from five-time Tour de France winner Lance Armstrong. Recovering from life-threatening cancer and training for his comeback to the Tour, Armstrong returned to Boone, North Carolina, the site of his earlier training. For the first time since the beginning of his long recovery, his joy in the bike, in himself, and in the mountains transcended the driving anger and competitiveness that had driven him before. "I passed the rest of the trip in a state of near-reverence for those beautiful, peaceful, soulful mountains. The rides were demanding and quiet, and I rode with a pure love of the bike, until Boone began to feel like the Holy Land to me, a place I had come to on a pilgrimage."

I believe the joy of this pilgrimage is available to all of us. For the afternoon bike rider, it's the glide down a long hill or the gentle turnings of a leafy bike trail. For the swimmer, it's the plunge, the glide, and the long strokes. For the journal keeper, it's opening to a new page and writing the date and the first few words of private thoughts. For the bird watcher, it's the arrival of a tanager. For the home repair aficionado, it's putting the finishing touches on a renovated room.

Although it sounds simple, it's not so easy if you have performance addiction. Can you enjoy the bike ride without beating your previous time trial, or weighing yourself before and afterward? Can you swim to the point of enjoyment and not a moment longer, even if you've done fewer laps than the last time? Can you keep a journal without comparing yourself to a best-selling novelist? Can you enjoy the glimpse of a tanager without logging on to a Web site to see whether it breaks a record for early arrival? Can you look around a room that you've just refinished without noting a dozen flaws in your own work?

I hope you'll try. If you can take pleasure in the action without the judgment, the enjoyment without the measurement, and the experience without the evaluation, you'll know what it feels like to escape performance addiction.

What You Can Do about Performance Addiction

If you answered yes to the questions at the beginning of this chapter, a few important steps can bring significantly more joy to your life.

Do you experience joy only when you are impressing others with your wit and charm?

WRITING ASSIGNMENT: Write a thank-you note to someone who has made an important difference in your life. Don't even think about whether to send the note. Just try to be as complete as possible in your appreciation and praise. Tell that person what he or she has meant to you and why the relationship is so important to you.

Do you seldom find meaning in solitary activities?

WRITING ASSIGNMENT: The next time you start a new project on the job or at home, take a short break and list all the things you enjoy about what you're doing. Be as specific as possible. Can you identify where the enjoyment comes from? Ask yourself whether there are more projects of this kind that you would enjoy no matter what the outcomes.

Do you find meaning in the outcomes of situations but seldom in the process?

WRITING ASSIGNMENT: Describe twenty of your best moments. Distinguish between the moments when you've experienced performance addiction satisfaction—for example, awards, compliments from others, money, material purchases—and universal moments of joy. List experiences that people cherish such as the birth of a child, falling in love, seeing an old friend after years of absence, or a special musical experience.

10

Parenting and Performance Addiction

1. Do you want your children to be as competitive as you are?

2. Do you use their achievements to bolster your self-worth?

3. Do you frequently comment on your children's appearance?

4. Can you tolerate their lives taking a different course from what you have planned for them?

5. How much do you emphasize the need for academic or athletic success?

I THINK WE HAVE A LEGACY PROBLEM. And it's getting worse. The men and women who come to me and talk about performance addiction are reaching out not only to me, their parents, spouses, friends, and lovers but also to their children. I say reaching out, but they can't find them. Where are those children? Why do they seem so far away?

I talk to the driven, educated high achievers who postponed childbearing until their careers could be established, their finances were rock solid, and their accomplishments were assured. I talk to men who have been struggling for years to find time to spend with their children, who now discover that the children are grown and communication seems incomparably more difficult. There are parents whose relationships with their children are built almost exclusively on schedules, measurements, and performance objectives. Others find themselves confronting disappointment with the way their children have failed to live up to their potential.

Having children, caring for them, and committing to their future is a major project, and the parents who are well meaning far outnumber those who are indifferent. But many are profoundly uneasy about their relationships with their children. In some cases, today's parents are feeling that they have lost or are losing an immense opportunity.

Whether or not you are actually a parent, I think it is critical to understand our relationship to the coming generation and to appreciate what we are communicating to them. If you have children, you know how much their attitudes and behavior not only reflect your own but also remind you of your own relationship with your parents and other family members.

If you are not a parent, you still know what I'm talking about. Your relationship with your own parents is a living part of you, and you make daily choices about how you relate to them. We are all looking for love. If we recognize that the love given to us has been measured according to our performance rating, we have choices to make about whether we perpetuate that tradition by using the performance addiction system of measuring the attention that we give to others. Can the cycle be broken?

I'm referring to a reallocation of hours and responsibilities. I don't necessarily mean moms and dads spending more time playing catch or video games with their sons and daughters. I wonder, however, if we sometimes lose sight of children through the haze of criteria, measurements, tests, and anxieties that tend to distort their images.

If you have performance addiction and you don't want your children to have it, how can you break the cycle? All of us need to sweep away the illusions that we have lived with in our own

lives—illusions about the way happiness, rewards, and fulfillment are supposed to come with success, prosperity, and achievement, and illusions about the way we can find love and give it in
return. If we pass those on to the next generation without knowing who our children are and listening to their needs, our legacy
will be flawed.

Looking for Balance

Parents often have preconceived notions about how they would
like their children's lives to turn out. They worry about what will
happen if their children don't measure up to expectations. But
children need unconditional love from their parents, even if they
can't articulate those needs themselves. In one of my groups, a
mother was able to discover how her performance addiction was
hurting her daughters. The news, however, came from outside the
family.

ANITA: LEARNING HOW A DAUGHTER FEELS

Anita has three daughters she loves unequivocally and with
unstinting devotion. Helen, now nineteen, is her only child by
her first marriage. The other girls, by her second husband, are
twelve and ten.

Anita was raised in a strict, religious home. Her parents are
Mormons, and her father, a high school football coach, never
approved of his daughter or the men she married. In both
marriages, Anita found men who were remote, judgmental,
and demanding. She knows exactly how to win acceptance
from her present husband, who is a research scientist for the
government. When she is impeccably dressed and made up,
looking much younger than her forty-six years, she has his
full approval. But if she reveals any signs of aging, his disapproval is palpable. So she is constantly working on her

appearance. The surgical improvements have included breast implants, a stomach tuck, and cosmetic surgery on her chin and forehead. With relentless exercise and deprivation, she seems intent on looking like a model. Her husband approves.

Anita worries constantly about her daughters' grades, academic standing, and athletic achievements. She's distressed when one of them is in trouble or falls behind. In group, she expresses concern about how the girls are doing.

One evening, another member of Anita's group, Lillian, starts to talk about her relationship with her own mother. Up to now, Anita and Lillian seemed to have very little in common. Lillian and her husband have no children, and the issues that she's dealing with seem far removed from Anita and her world.

Lillian is a professional singer whose preoccupations seem focused on her status and accomplishments in the musical community. Anita has her obsessive concerns about her daughters' achievements and her husband's approval. She has her compulsions about disguising her age and altering her appearance. Lillian, by contrast, has abiding concerns about talent, performance ability, and standing among professional musicians. Where's the link?

Lillian is the youngest of three sisters. When Anita begins to talk about her girls, Lillian relates immediately. She can tell Anita about her own mother. Lillian describes a woman who had a remote relationship with her husband and devoted herself entirely to Lillian and her two sisters.

"I love my mother," Lillian tells us. "But I have never felt free to live without worrying about how I would affect her." She goes on to describe how that feeling has inhibited her sense of freedom and her enjoyment of her own life and career. It even played a role in her decision not to have children, since she didn't want to pass along these concerns to others.

It's a remarkable moment, as if one of Anita's children, now twenty years older, were speaking to her mother about the consequences of her performance addiction. On Lillian's side, there is the opportunity to tell Anita what it's like to bear the weight of a mother's expectations. It's as if Lillian has taken the side of Anita's daughters and is campaigning for their freedom.

There are things about herself that Anita feels compelled to acknowledge—that she will never reach the high moral ground where her father will finally embrace her; that however much she devotes herself to exercise, cosmetic surgery, and grooming, she can never meet the criteria of beauty that seem to satisfy her husband. But she has a choice. Will she allow her preoccupation with her daughters' performance become the sole way by which she measures her own sense of self? Lillian is trying to save Anita and her daughters from this burden.

What are the illusions for Anita? That she will prove her worthiness to her father by raising granddaughters he could be proud of? There is the illusion that the girls' success will allow her husband to reward Anita for doing well by giving her unstinting affection. There is also the illusion that the success of her daughters will be a fully satisfying culmination of their own desires and ambitions. Anita wishes happiness for these girls as much as she wishes success.

Anita is shocked to realize that however well her children succeed, they will still want her love rather than her anxiety. Years from now, they will continue to wonder what they have to do to gain her approval and affection, and how they can compensate for their own failure to achieve the heights of accomplishment that she dreamed possible for them. Unless Anita can deal with her own performance addiction, her daughters will feel the way Lillian does about her mother. Anita's daughters, however much they may love their mother, will never live freely without worrying how their lives will affect her.

High-Grade Unhappiness

I sometimes wonder what parents would think if I informed them that their most accomplished children were going to end up unhappy. What if they knew that children who inherit their criteria of success can become victims of confusion, addiction, and lack of self-esteem?

The evidence comes from Dr. Armand Nicoli, a Harvard psychiatrist who has taught a course for thirty years called "Sigmund Freud and C. S. Lewis: Two Contrasting Worldviews." Among the core courses at Harvard, this has been rated number one for the past four years. For the past eleven years, it has been included in the curriculum at Harvard Medical School, and it is the topic of a PBS special. During one class, Dr. Nicoli poses a simple question: "Are Harvard students happy?"

The students hem and haw. But invariably the class consensus is that Harvard students are, in fact, quite the opposite.

Dr. Nicoli feigns surprise. "What? How can that be? You have every need satisfied! You have food prepared for you, a place to sleep. You have intelligence, youth, a bright future."

The discussion proceeds from there. Dr. Nicoli's students arrive at the conclusion that "many Harvard students are not happy because Harvard is a lonely place and because they do not have meaningful relationships."

With that rueful admission out of the way, the real discussion in Dr. Nicoli's class begins. Where does your concept of happiness come from? What does it mean to be successful and how is that related to happiness? In a place where intellectual pursuits are paramount, what will be the rewards of your extraordinary efforts?

Dr. Nicoli has been encouraging such discussion for years, and he knows where it will lead. "Their concept of success is fame and fortune," he says. "They believe that someday they'll be successful—and that's when they'll be happy. Yet they concur that intellectual pursuits alone do not make for good, effective people."

Returning to my fantasy of clearing away the illusions of performance addiction, I imagine what an education it would be for the parents of those students to also be present in Dr. Nicoli's classroom. After all, their children have reached the pinnacle of the Ivy League and all it has to offer. Considering all the cost and effort required to deliver their sons and daughters to this renowned institution of higher learning, what if these parents could hear Dr. Nicoli questioning the very set of performance measures that were used to assess their children? Parents with performance addiction would be aghast.

The Legacy Question

In a world where success is sacred, can we really reject the measurements of achievement and the certification of intellectual rigor that seemingly promise such bountiful rewards? It's tough.

Suppose you did warn students accepted at Harvard that they might not be happy there. Of course, this would be a sweeping generalization, but what if it were true in the majority of cases? Even if they believed you, they would not believe the notion that Harvard will not open doors to a rewarding future. I talk to parents who have been raised in an atmosphere of performance addiction, who convey the same ideals and values to their children, and they simply do not believe me. Often when I can ask a mother or father to describe their son or daughter, I get an evaluation that focuses on academic achievement, athletic prowess, awards, prospects, and aspirations. In this melange of evaluative criteria, the child is lost. I don't understand the relationship. I don't know what delights have been discovered in this child or even what the parent has learned from being a parent. It is as if the resumé started at birth and is gradually being filled in and refined by the child's existence. But when this happens, there is a loss. And it is just as much the parent's as it is the child's.

KATE AND JIM: COMPETING VIEWS OF HAPPINESS

Kate is married with three children. Both Jim and Kate went to Boston College, where they met as seniors, and Kate went on to get her MBA. She gave up a lucrative job at a bank to become a full-time mother. Jim is an attorney who just made partner in his firm. Upon reaching that long-sought-after goal, he made himself miserable comparing his income to that of partners in other firms around the city.

Sixteen-year-old Melinda is an all-state soccer player but an average student. The younger girls, ages eight and five, are what Kate calls "developmentally challenged." Kate concluded that she needed to leave her job and stay home because "the two youngest have so many problems."

Kate and Jim are far different people than they were when they first met. With a smile, Kate describes both of them as "nerdy." "We were both focused—we knew exactly what we expected." She adds, "Life has not been as we expected."

In Kate's description of the family dynamics, it becomes clear that Jim is focused on the eldest daughter, the champion soccer player, Melinda. He is after Melinda to bring up her grades. If she does that and an admissions committee factors in her soccer skills, she will have a good shot at top schools. So Jim is constantly on her case about doing her homework. She resists, of course, and is outraged when she is asked to look after her two sisters. Kate recounts one explosion where Melinda screamed, "Am I supposed to be their second mother?"

Jim concentrates on Melinda because she offers the greatest promise. But there are two other girls in the family! Jim cannot deal with his own frustration. One Saturday, when Kate left the younger girls home with Jim for just a few hours, she returned to discover that he had thrown a tantrum. A few minutes into lunch, eight-year-old Gillian made a food request that Dad couldn't handle. He sent her to her room, and when her younger sister began bawling, he dismissed both of them for the rest of the afternoon. When Kate returned, both girls were in their rooms and Jim was working on his computer.

In fact, Jim has simply eliminated the two youngest girls from the equation. He doesn't ask them about their schoolwork. He doesn't read to them. This doesn't work for Kate. The youngest ones seem the happiest while Melinda always seems stressed out and is the most confrontational. But where does Kate herself fit into this family? She was a star achiever in her own day. Will her two youngest daughters live up to her example?

At last, Kate has arrived at the point where she is willing to stop measuring her two younger daughters by their accomplishments. Jim, however, is still focused on Melinda. What has become of the other two girls? Have they disappeared?

Kate embraces them and loves them. Their joy in living reminds her of her older brother, an artist who has never worried about the "right" career. She makes the contrast with her husband, who is a constant critic of his own achievements and makes himself miserable by comparing himself to others.

Jim is still hoping against hope that the other two girls will somehow "recover" from their deficiencies. These daughters may or may not become the daughters that he had wished for. But he has a choice: Will he become a father to the daughters he actually has who clearly crave his affection, or will he perpetuate the tradition of the absent parent?

I do not mean to suggest even for a moment that financial, social, and professional pressures are illusory. Both Jim and Kate know that Jim cannot neglect his job, having made partner, to spend more time with his daughters. The fact that his younger daughters need additional help both in and out of school means the financial pressures are greater. Soon Jim and Kate may be looking at private schools for these children, with the vast costs that are entailed. Even if the young girls are not high achievers, their development will never be neglected by their conscientious parents.

Wherever they show a glimmer of promise, no expense will be spared in assisting them to live up to their potential. In fact, his daughters' situation has made Jim more aware of his family's financial requirements and dependence on him as provider.

The path that led to his current position was not an easy one, and a simple remark or observation can easily pique the envy he feels toward other partners who seem far more confident, contented, and certainly better paid than he is. In this respect, his two younger daughters remind him of his own vulnerability. Deep in the recesses of his anxiety and unease, he wonders whether he, too, is held back by some kind of learning difficulty. That thought disturbs him, and as Kate can see, it makes his daughters' difficulties all the more problematic for him.

The Parenting Trap

The choices that many parents have to make are quite intense and even unfair. I am reminded of Chris, a client I had for many years, who worked in the upper echelons of a high-tech company.

CHRIS: GIVING UP HIS LIFE FOR THE JOB OF A LIFETIME

Chris lives with his wife and two sons in an affluent suburb of Boston, but he is obliged by his job to make weekly trips to California. He leaves on Sunday morning and returns on Thursday.

Now his sons are in high school. Chris's wife wants a change. She wants him home during the week. The boys need him. She needs him. How long must she put up with his weekly absences?

Hoping to find a solution that will work for the entire family, Chris interviews for a job in Phoenix, Arizona, with a rival company that has been pursuing him for some time. The salary and benefits will be far more than what he's making now. Once the family moves to Phoenix, he won't have to travel. He'll be able to spend more time with his sons. With less time away, he imagines he'll be far more attentive to his family.

But suddenly there's a snag. His wife declares she doesn't want to move. She knows him too well. They will buy a huge house, live in absolute luxury, have all the amenities, and before long Chris will be spending days and nights at work and she will be home with the boys. It was bad enough not to see him all week. In Arizona, she foresees that she and the boys will be even more alone cut off from family and friends.

Chris has a painful interview with the CEO of the Phoenix company. The offer is on the table—"unbelievable money, stock options, the whole nine yards." Then Chris breaks the news that his wife doesn't want to move. The CEO leans across the table. "Don't be foolish," he says to Chris. "This is the chance of a lifetime. It will never happen again. You know, there are plenty of women down here. You can always get another wife."

This is the real world of our high-paid performers. The words of the CEO may seem shocking but only because the sentiments are so boldly stated. Whether explicit or implicit, these are the choices that the most successful individuals in our society are making every day. The CEO merely stated the accepted ethic: relationships are secondary to material and professional pursuit.

Chris turned down the offer.

We can choose or not choose to subscribe to that ethic. We can't make the choices go away.

The Preparation Process

If we can't change the realities of society's demands, how can we prepare our children to cope with the exigencies they're going to face?

If we have succeeded throughout our lives by meeting measurements of performance and making increasingly large demands on ourselves, how do we break the pattern, and when is it necessary to do so? What's called for? A dramatic lifestyle change? A new vision of our shared future? Clever escape routes? More time off? Ingenious new forms of time management and instant relaxation? More efficient ways to discover quality time with spouses, friends, family, and children?

All these methods are being tried, of course. The frenzy of busyness has reached a crescendo where people are truly experiencing a sense of crisis. As we witness CEOs of leading companies gripped by their need to outperform, blindly driven by forces that erase all semblance of ethical or personal responsibility, we don't have to be told that something is seriously amiss. As consumption soars to excesses that are far beyond the reasonable needs of rational individuals, and as acquisitiveness reaches the proportions of a great hunger, we don't need any further statistics to prove that our ravenous appetites are out of control.

If you don't have the power to halt the acceleration of demands, reverse the accumulation of goods, or mastermind a new appreciation for humane values, what can you do? I would contend that each of us can recognize and come to grips with our performance addiction. It is a far greater challenge than rescheduling work routines, reorganizing free time, or redirecting energies toward new activities. Although more challenging, it is also more rewarding. If we recognize performance addiction in ourselves, if we see where it comes from and how it causes us to act, then we have an opportunity to change the legacy we leave to our children, students, coworkers, and spouses.

Balanced living cannot be achieved by rescheduling or retooling. I believe we can achieve it only by knowing who we are and what is driving us—and, perhaps most difficult of all, by allowing and helping others to understand how we and they can cope with those forces.

The Teaching Child

How well do we tolerate and cope with our imperfections? Children can sometimes be our teachers in this matter. They often have a surprisingly natural way of constructively dealing with vulnerabilities whereas we, as parents, tend to complicate the process. This was vividly illustrated for me by Liam, one of my clients, who gained wisdom from his son's ability to appraise himself realistically.

LIAM: LEARNING FROM HIS SON

Having known Liam for a number of months, I have come to expect that he will miss about half his appointments. He'll call at the last minute to say he has an unexpected assignment and needs to work late. It gives me a sample of what his family experiences. A highly positioned manager in an accounting firm, by nature a perfectionist, Liam makes excessive demands on himself, leaving nothing to chance.

Not surprisingly, his ten-year-old son, Jason, is fraught with performance anxiety to a degree that often makes him fearful around other people. Liam and I have discussed the many ways that he might talk to his son about his own perfectionistic expectations and how they can get in the way. I believe that father and son are so much alike that they have a great deal to gain by sharing. Liam is resolved to have more realistic conversations with Jason. Rather than trying to project a flawless image of himself, perhaps Liam can help Jason understand how his father's work causes him anxiety and how—in similar ways—Jason's school performance creates discomfort for the boy.

With the help of a psychologist, Jason prepared for a piano recital. The boy was understandably nervous before the recital. Afterward, Liam told me it went reasonably well, but his son made mistakes. Unbeknownst to Jason, his parents purchased a videotape of the performance. Liam decided he'd better not let Jason know about the tape. After all, what if he heard all the mistakes he made? Liam speculated (and projected) that perhaps his son would be so torn apart by hearing his errors that he would never want to perform again.

Jason found out about the tape and insisted on viewing it.

"I watched it with him," Liam said. "I could feel my heart race. I could imagine the humiliation he felt."

But Liam was wrong.

At the tape's conclusion, Jason turned to his father and said, "It wasn't so bad, Dad. I won't worry about it so much next time. It was just my second recital."

Liam was floored. How could his son have this kind of perspective about his performance?

"I don't imagine it came easily," I suggested.

It is quite clear this is the kind of perspective that Liam does not have on his own work. Jason is way ahead of his father. How will Liam find the resources to deal with his own anxiety? Where will father and son go from here?

Ironically, Jason had to go outside his home to discover perspective when his own father could have told him volumes about dealing with anxiety. To Jason, who hears only lectures from his father, it must seem as if Liam performs flawlessly at work, never worries about doing well, and never experiences uncertainty. Once again I encourage Liam to tell his son the truth about himself and his work, instead of making it sound like a piece of cake. "Tell him some of your doubts, your anxiety. Let him in on your real internal dialogue."

I imagine what it would be like for them to share their problems and strategize together. Can Liam tell his own truth about performance and competency, and, I hope, pass along this knowledge to his son? This is what he would like to do, and gradually he is getting there.

Buying These Wonderful Myths

So many myths crowd our thinking so early. Some are implanted in childhood. Others are accepted on probation, and it's only later that we realize we have accepted them wholeheartedly—for instance, the myth that accomplishment leads to fulfillment, even if you're motivated by performance addiction, or that discipline makes you stronger, even if it's obsessive and driven by perfectionism.

Intellectually, it is easy enough to dispel these myths. We have statistics to show that smart, rich people are not necessarily happier, nor do they feel more secure. We can convince ourselves that many well-to-do high achievers feel no more fulfilled and accomplished than people who have perfectly ordinary jobs and average incomes. We fully appreciate the wisdom of great platitudes like "Wealth does not buy happiness" and "Beauty is only skin deep." We can even acknowledge that the immeasurable qualities inherent in character represent something far stronger than the rigors of self-discipline.

But we also know that achievement, wealth, and beauty can be positive attributes if we are not being driven by performance addiction. There are attractive, affluent people who achieve great things and who place their attributes in proper perspective. They don't expect love and respect to be earned exclusively by the impressiveness of their resumes.

How can you enjoy your achievements without the compulsive need to do more and be more? We all need some reformative experiences that reshape our thinking. How do we search for happiness? The answer, I believe, is in balanced living.

What You Can Do about Performance Addiction

If you are a parent, here are some insights that may help you deal with performance addiction issues in your family. These issues are equally important to educators, counselors, and others who have close contact with children.

Do you want your children to be as competitive as you are?

INSIGHT: You can encourage competitiveness without trying to fulfill your own ego needs. If children are just beginning to enjoy competitive activities, pay attention to the ones that seem most satisfying. Do they truly enjoy trying to win or achieve, or are they doing it to try to gain your love? It is important to let your child know that your love and respect will be unconditional, but you will support the child's endeavors if winning is important to him or her.

Do you use their achievements to bolster your self-worth?

INSIGHT: When children are young, it's important to support their natural inclinations even if you can't see the connection to outcomes or achievements. Try to separate your own wishes from what your child wants to do. Can you allow your daughter to express herself physically without being preoccupied with her looks? (For example: If your daughter wants to go outside and run around, do you insist she must fix her hair first?) Can you allow your son to engage in activities you consider nonmasculine without feeling uneasy and interfering? (For example: He wants to quit Little League and take drama lessons.)

When you talk with your child, it's important to do more listening than talking. Try to be aware of the differences between you and your child, particularly differences that are upsetting to you. These are the areas where your expectations for your child are most likely to create undue pressure.

Do you frequently comment on your child's appearance?

INSIGHT: List all the positive aspects about your child's appearance that catch your attention. Include articles of clothing as well as positive physical attributes. At least once a week, mention a specific positive attribute. For instance, you might mention, "You're really wearing a sunny smile this morning" or "That's a neat cap. I love the color!" Be sure to make your comments as specific as possible.

Avoid making critical remarks about appearance or watering down your compliments. Positive messages can be diluted or even poisoned if you add a negative. If you say, "You've looked gloomy all week, so I'm glad to see you smiling," your child will probably register the criticism and forget the compliment. Avoid critical observations. "That's a neat cap—I wish you'd wear it the right way" is more likely to start an argument than reinforce your child's positive feelings.

Can you tolerate their lives taking a different course from what you have planned for them?

INSIGHT: Describe to yourself or in a journal the lifestyle your son or daughter could lead that would bother you the most. Include every aspect that you consider important such as schooling, curriculum choices, location, marriage or relationships, and income. Be as detailed as possible. (For example: "I couldn't stand my child going to college in the South, or majoring in philosophy, or marrying an Irish Catholic, or living in Rhode Island, or working as a middle school teacher, or never going to graduate school, or earning less than $60,000 a year.)

Next, evaluate whether you have legitimate reasons for your concerns. Upon reflection, can you determine which concerns are based on your own biases, insecurities, or unresolved disappointments?

How much do you emphasize the need for academic or athletic success?

INSIGHT: Depending on the age of your child, this might be a good time to evaluate your interaction and alter the ways you try to direct his or her future decision or actions. Here are some warning signs that you may be directing your child to follow the course that you determine, rather than discovering his or her own way.

- Are you trying to steer your child on a course that would be exciting to you? (For example: "Johnny, you are going to make a great lawyer. I can just tell by the way you think!")

- Perhaps you tend to answer for your children when they are asked what they want to be when they grow up.

- If your child is participating in activities (soccer, drama, etc.), evaluate whether he or she is doing it for the love of the activity or to win your love.

11

Balancing Work
and Life

DO YOU FEEL THAT WORK is running you ragged? If so, it's necessary for you to address your performance addiction and take important steps to achieve balanced living.

A number of times in this book, I have mentioned the group therapy sessions where men and women discuss work and life issues. A recurrent theme in these meetings is familiar to anyone who has dealt with alcoholism, drug addiction, eating disorders, or any other kind of addictive behavior. That theme is old patterns.

For most of the individuals in these groups, the old patterns do not relate to alcohol, drugs, or food. Rather, they are patterns of performance addiction. The most serious issues revolve around the balance between work and every other aspect of life. People make resolutions to spend more time with their families, to get to know their spouses, to appreciate their children, then a few weeks later confess that they have returned to working fifteen-hour days. Or they've started new, intense projects to fill their "spare time." Or they haven't followed through on their resolutions. They haven't reached out to parents, their spouses are beginning to give up on them again, and work obligations are yanking them away from their children.

As they work harder and longer, taking on one obligation after another, they find that they are grappling with old patterns. These patterns stir up the feelings that brought them into group in the first place: unhappiness, emptiness, alienation, and despair. As the groups continue to meet, week after week, members begin to regard the group itself as their island of opportunity. It is at least one place where empathy is more important than accomplishment. All these hardworking people are trying valiantly to rearrange their pursuit of perfection into something that brings them a greater degree of happiness. The group members are searching for some of the ingredients that were missing from their own families and childhood experiences. They are in the process of discovering what brings love and respect.

Wealth and accomplishments have not delivered what they needed, so they have embarked on a search for something else. As one member of the group talks about his performance addiction, the others empathize. They know the forces that are driving him. They are dealing with the same issues. As they listen, I see a sense of calmness come over the faces of these very driven, perfectionistic people. Seeing themselves in others and revealing more of themselves to each other, they are beginning to discover what has been missing.

When I intervene, it is to add a very important ingredient: urgency. There is a simple but important phrase I want them to consider when they talk about what they intend to do next: "before it's too late."

Leo: A Tacit Misunderstanding

Leo began working in the family's commercial real estate business when he was twenty-two years old and had just graduated from college. When I first met him, he was in his mid-thirties with all the symptoms of high stress. He was drinking too much and unable to sleep. I thought he looked much older than his age. He said he "hated the business." He complained of cutthroat competition, resented the business-focused socializing, and chafed at the relentless haggling involved in closing every deal. He talked about the problems that kept him awake at night. Leo's main concern was his inability to free himself from the business. He couldn't just up and leave, he insisted. It would disappoint his father too much.

Leo struck me as a very physical, high-energy person. He had been a star athlete in high school and was still in excellent shape. A tireless worker, he often stayed on the job seven days a week, working until six o'clock or later, then having dinner with clients. Every week he would come bounding up the steep stairs to my office, exactly on time for his appointment.

As much as he wanted to liberate himself from the constant demands of the business, he could not find a way. He was the oldest son in his Greek-American family and felt he would be letting the others down if he "deserted" his father. Yet he also knew he was pushing himself too hard. He was always uncomfortable at the obligatory dinners where he had to wine and dine clients. On those occasions, he drank heavily, which wasn't good news when he had to drive himself home. On at least one occasion, he had fallen asleep at the wheel. He woke up before hitting a guard rail, swerving just in time to avoid disaster. But he shrugged off the dangers. "That's just part of the game," he told me.

As Leo talked to me about his family's demands, I asked him to describe his father. From Leo's initial description, I thought his father was strong, steady, and indefatigable. But as Leo revealed more about the family, I saw that he had given me an erroneous first impression. This father was not quite the pillar of strength whom Leo had first portrayed. In fact, Leo's father suffered from depression and at one point had been hospitalized. In fact, Leo observed, he found it very difficult to talk to his father about anything. "He's very sensitive."

Over the weeks, I could see that Leo's pressure to perform

had lessened only slightly. One night he said, "Doc, I'm in prison. I hate doing this. I want out. But I will never be able to tell my dad."

I suggested a meeting with his father. Leo said he would think about it. In the meantime, I was becoming very concerned. "Leo, I can see you're taking chances. You're sleep deprived. You're working fifteen-hour days, seven days a week. If you're going to drink at these dinners, you've got to get someone else to drive you home."

He cautioned me not to overreact. "I've been working like this for years. I'll get through one more summer. Then I'll talk to my dad about getting out."

Six days after that conversation, I received a call from Leo's wife. When the accident happened, he had been driving alone. This time he had not wakened in time to miss the guard rail.

"They took him to Boston," his wife told me. "He's in surgery now."

Leo is paraplegic. He will never walk again. His father, now seventy years old, has been unable to manage the company without him.

Months after the accident, Leo came in and told me about the belated conversation that he'd had with his father. When they finally talked about the "damn business," Leo discovered that his father had been wanting to get out of it himself for years but had been afraid to say anything. After all, he knew how hard Leo was working—how he "poured his heart and soul" into making the business a success. Leo's father had thought it would be a crushing blow if he decided to sell out.

"It's time to let go," Leo's father had told him. "It's caused us all too much pain."

Telling me this, Leo shook his head. There was a long moment of silence.

"After all this, Doc," said Leo, "I never told my father it was me who wanted out."

The Costs of Addiction

Leo's story is true. Do you have to prove yourself to someone? If so, how hard will you work? How much will you push yourself? What risks will you take? What if it turns out that you don't want to prove yourself at all?—that you only want to be accepted, or loved, or forgiven?

I can't tell you the exact steps to take because everyone's challenges and dilemmas are unique. But I can tell you about the important choices I have seen people make to create a better legacy for themselves, their parents, their spouses, and their children. Will these steps work for you? I hope that you'll consider them, then decide for yourself.

CAL: LEARNING TO USE THE DIMMER SWITCH

In many of my discussions with Cal, we have talked about him learning how to use the dimmer switch. It is an ability that he needs to develop because he has always been entirely turned on or off with nothing in between. The president and CEO of his own company, he can quite easily be engulfed by his work, only to emerge after weeks or months to discover that he has been abusing his health, that relationships have deteriorated, and that once again he has been unable to find a balance between his emotional needs and the all-consuming demands of his business.

What he has done: Every Sunday night, Cal has begun taking inventory. "I ask myself if I exercised regularly, ate reasonably, and slept enough. Did I nurture my relationships? If I answer yes to these questions, then I feel my intensity for work is okay. It is balanced in a way it has never been in my life."

When Cal goes through a week where he "starts to take ordinary things for granted," this Sunday-night inventory brings him up short. He is reminded of discussions we've had about the way he categorizes ordinary things. In the past, this categorization became a way of measuring out his own valuable time and pigeonholing other people and events in his life. And he reminds himself: "If everyone could do these ordinary things, what a different world it would be."

As Cal does his Sunday-night inventory and works on his dimmer switch, his own view of himself begins to change. "I always thought I had to hit the grand slam to be somebody. Now I am slowly realizing that my preoccupation with greatness really distorted my view of the ordinary. In fact, I don't even think of the daily self-care items as being ordinary anymore. That's a great change for me."

Will it work for you? A weekly inventory might be the perfect place to begin, particularly if you identify with the way Cal gets sucked into his work. It may help you control your dimmer switch.

Look at the ordinary things in the way that Cal does. A one-hour walk is just about as ordinary as you can get. You need it for yourself. Washing dishes and putting things away in the kitchen are pretty ordinary endeavors. You and your spouse may do this together. A child's band concert is not going to enrich your musical appreciation. But you'll feel good and your child will be happy to have you there.

Scheduling issues may seem like an old problem—too much to do and not enough time. But that's exactly why Cal's Sunday-night inventory might help. You can get better control over your dimmer switch, adjusting and balancing so that you rule your own choices and are not ruled by performance addiction.

JODIE: DECLARING HER LOVE BEFORE IT'S TOO LATE

"My father loved me so much when I was a cute little girl," Jodie recalls. She, in turn, idolized him. "I would follow him everywhere. When he cut the grass, I would be right there behind him with my little mower, literally walking in his footsteps." That all changed when she became "an adolescent with a mind of my own," according to Jodie. "He wanted nothing to do with me. He even refused to come to my wedding. No man was ever good enough."

The disapproval and withholding of love and respect became a formative part of Jodie's performance addiction. Twice divorced and remarried, she has clearly "moved up." She is now married to a doctor whom she thought her father would like, but she is miserable. The breach between Jodie and her father has seemed beyond resolution. Nothing she's done is good enough, and even now that she has finally found a husband who should be acceptable, she cannot win the approval she needs from the father she once adored.

What she has done: Now in his eighties, Jodie's father was admitted to the hospital with pains in his chest. He had suffered a mild heart attack. On the long, anxious drive to the hospital, Jodie found that she experienced feelings that seemed to make light of all the years of resentment and rebellion. Winning her father's approval faded in importance. She just wanted him alive. "I finally realized I really love him," she said. "I could never live up to his image of me, but I now realize that is his limitation. It really doesn't have much to do with me."

Sitting at her father's bedside while he drifted in and out, Jodie found herself thinking about her father's family. "He got very little from his folks. He had no idea how to relate to me." The hours passed, and when he was fully awake, Jodie told him how much she loved him. She could not say those words without crying. "For the first time in my memory as an adult, he thanked me for coming," Jodie told me. "And he said in his typical, angry voice that he loved me also."

Will it work for you? To the degree that performance addiction is tied in with perfectionism, it sends us down the wrong pathway. We hope against hope that being good enough will finally put us on the road to gaining the love of a parent, a spouse, or a boss. But the opposite of perfectionism is acceptance. If our behavior or performance has never been acceptable to others, it is unlikely that we will be acceptable to ourselves.

There's a part of Jodie's experience that might work for you. Perhaps you need to think about your ability to accept *as people* the figures from whom you have hoped to win love, respect, or approval. All are imperfect, limited, restrained, and molded by their own experiences. They can never give you as much emotional support as you would probably like to get from them, but this is the reality of their character, not a shortcoming of yours. One thing is certain, however: If you focus on living up to their expectations, your judgment will be distorted by performance addiction. When we perceive parents, bosses, or any authority figures as judgmental gods, we live in fear of their wrath. And balanced living is impossible if fear dogs our footsteps.

MAUREEN: FINDING ACCEPTANCE OUTSIDE THE PROFESSIONAL CIRCLE

Like many talented people who must spend hours in rehearsal or practice, Maureen has her demons. A cellist in a symphony orchestra, she was an only child who showed early promise. Her parents spared nothing to make sure that she had the best teachers and training. Her early pleasure in the instrument—the simple gratification of having something she could do very well—began to diminish as the pressures intensified. By the time Maureen was accepted at the prestigious Curtis Institute, she had not only studied with a demanding series of teachers but had spent many hours with psychiatrists to help her deal with performance anxiety, with orthopedists to diagnose various joint problems, and with tutors to help her sustain her grades while maintaining her grueling rehearsal schedule.

What she has done: In the group that Maureen has joined where performance addiction is a common theme, she finds herself among people who do not want to coach her toward perfection. Unlike all the parents, teachers, and coaches with whom she has dealt, the members of this intimate group do not give a hoot if she can perform better. No one in the group is working to help her to conquer her performance anxiety. In fact, we don't know much about her world at all. We just know Maureen. It's the one safety zone in her performance-addicted life. If she never played another note, she could come back and find people she values and who care about who she is. Or she could tour all the capitals of the world as a soloist only to find upon her return that the people in this group are far more concerned about her life, her love, and her happiness than about her reviews.

This group involvement has helped Maureen to create a new relationship to her vocation. "Every once in a while," she tells us, "on rare occasions, I just lose myself in my music." As she tries to describe this, I think of the flow state, where no one is judging, no one is watching the scoreboard, and no one is keeping time. She describes becoming so involved that she stops thinking about how she is performing. It is a completely intense experience untainted by performance anxiety. She is simply playing. As rarely as it happens, Maureen now feels that she knows what she wants to capture. "Maybe this is the key."

Will it work for you? Watch a child who is just beginning to wield a crayon, toot a horn, or discover a magnet, and I think you can recapture the sense of what it means to be in the process of learning. It is a process of discovery. Improvement is possible but not necessary. Nothing is being rated. No one is expecting perfection. Later, when there's constant assessment, it spoils the learning process. It turns an enjoyable opportunity into a burden. But if you can capture the process of learning, you will find release. And once it's rediscovered, you will have a better way to make choices about what you do and how you do it.

It is natural to gravitate toward things that give us pleasure. When the pleasure of learning has been lost, we may easily forget what drew us there in the first place. Yet we need to experience that pleasure for balanced living. As Maureen discovered, maybe it is the key.

HAROLD: FINDING HIS FAMILY TIES

Harold feels like a man held captive by his work. He is a well-paid and highly skilled manager of a product team. Typically, dinner is brought into the building at 7:30 P.M. "Everyone knows that if you're not there, you're not committed, and you won't be around for long." With eighty-hour workweeks, Harold is estranged from his family. A number of times he has threatened to quit unless something changes, but he says, "Every time I threaten to leave, I get a package of options thrown in front of me. And the lures are beautiful. The options are delivered when the project is completed or the product is marketable. If a manager sees a project through to completion, he wins big. If he doesn't, he won't get another shot at participating in the most interesting and challenging projects. They say, 'Stick with this project, Harold, and when the product goes to market, you'll cash in.'"

Harold says he can't walk away from the money, but he also says that's not the worst thing about his situation. "What is really killing me," he says, "is I use the same carrot with the people who work for me. When those guys want to walk away, I do the same thing to them that I hate my boss for. I dangle the money in their faces. I know they can't walk away. They're as driven as I am. I know their goals, their big dreams. I know I have them as long as I want them, and they will turn away from their families every time if I offer enough."

When Harold was growing up, his father relished telling his boys the notorious Vince Lombardi quote: "Winning isn't everything. It's the only thing." Needless to say, the message stuck with Harold, becoming his mantra and, currently, his curse. But the father who uttered those profoundly motivational sentiments had more than one child. He had five. The oldest daughter, Edith, is mentally retarded.

What he has done: Harold goes back to Cleveland to see his father and have a few beers with his brothers. They watch the Browns in action. But the important conversations have been with his sister. When Harold was growing up, she was an embarrassment. Harold's father tried to put as much distance between the "accomplished" children and his mentally challenged child, and his campaign was successful. "I knew what my father wanted of us," Harold recalls, "and to tell the truth, I thought he was right. Why shouldn't we excel? Why should any of us turn out like my sister? Honestly, I am ashamed to say, I avoided her. I was afraid to be embarrassed by her."

Harold and his sister talk more than they ever did as children, and he is beginning to take an active part in her care. This is bringing him closer to his own family, as his children start to learn about the Aunt Edith they never knew. His children are beginning to discover an aspect of their impossibly distant father that they never could have seen otherwise.

Will it work for you? Once you know the scene of the crime, any revisit will help you make discoveries about yourself. This is far from an exercise in Freudian ruminations. Rather, it is a way to discover some of the roots of performance addiction. If you want to understand why you do the things you do, it's essential to know where your behavior is rooted. Only then can you make conscious choices about your current relationships and future behavior.

Teresa: Accepting the Empathy She Never Expected

Teresa was halfway through her second year of law school when her father died. She took several days off for the funeral and to spend time with her family. It was the best she could do. Exams were coming up. Her classmates were already beginning to research job prospects. There was a chance that Teresa would make law review.

Above all, she felt this was what her father would have wanted her to do. In her family there were never excuses for not performing. She knew exactly what her father would say: "He would tell me to buckle down and do the work. He would tell me there was absolutely no circumstance that could justify my withdrawing." And her mother has much the same attitude. In her eyes, too, there are no excuses for failure.

Several months after her father's death, Teresa was struggling. She started to think about dropping out, and terror began to build. "I know I am so afraid my mother will be angry. I will lose her, too. I just can't stand the thought of her being mad with me. Feeling her disappointment seems unbearable."

Teresa's panic intensified when the dean asked her to come to the office. Throughout the weekend, Teresa's dread built to a crescendo. It was overlaid with the rage that her father would express when he was disappointed in her, his voice telling her, "You're a quitter, Teresa! Don't be a quitter!" And her mother saying, "There's no excuse for failure."

On Monday morning, there was no rage on the dean's face, not even a trace of reproach in her voice. "She was so understanding and kind, I just started crying," Teresa said. "Not even so much because she cared, but because I'd had two sleepless nights thinking how much I had disappointed her. It was *nothing* like that. She told me she knew I was an excellent student. She said, 'Teresa, sometimes life throws us a curve and we have to make adjustments.'"

What she has done: Teresa's meeting with the dean was alien to her prior experience with authority. That meeting, in fact, gave her a new opportunity to examine the flaws in her religion and to finally see the truth about what brings love and respect. She talked in amazement of how caring people had been. "I expected a repeat of what I experienced in my home, and it turned out just the opposite. I have wasted so much time trying to perfect myself to win people over, and all the while they just wanted me to be myself. It is so hard to believe that what I have been running from actually makes me more attractive."

Intellectually, she had understood that. But before she encountered someone who put Teresa first and her accomplishments second, Teresa lacked the life experience that could alter her belief system.

Will it work for you? None of us can manufacture an understanding dean, a kind teacher, an open-minded boss, or a nurturing mentor. Be sure to accept the wonderful occasions when they do appear. The relationships they have to offer may belie your preconceptions about authority figures and what they represent, but you have to be in a receptive state. The environment and preconditioning experiences that create performance addiction are so powerful that they often close off the possibility of relationships that do not involve evaluation and judgment.

When someone respects you for who you are rather than what you do, values your participation rather than your achievements, and accepts your limitations as well as your capabilities, the experience of that human bond is almost shocking. Under the tight reins of performance addiction, you have no freedom to be yourself, to fall down, and to reveal who you really are. But that can change. Well-meaning people are not simply those who watch you and judge you. They are also well-integrated people who can help you and care for you without forcing you to match preconceived expectations.

Coping well is not an answer. A number of group members told Teresa that they felt disconnected from her when she coped so well with the death of her father. They felt closer to her when they saw a truer picture: the young woman grieving for her father, trying to work full time, taking care of her mother, and going to law school at night. Then they could see someone recognizably human and utterly overwhelmed.

Perhaps the new interpersonal experiences are what you need for balanced living. You must have the willingness and openness to have these experiences, which means recognizing the roots and symptoms of your performance addiction. Discovering that there are people who will acknowledge who you are and what you need requires a great leap of faith.

Your Vitamin for Growth

The well-loved Boston psychoanalyst Elvin Semrad, who called sadness "the vitamin of growth," went on to say: "The only fuel for learning is the sadness you feel from your mistakes. It's important not to waste this fuel."

It may seem countermotivational that I should end this book by touching on sadness, but I think there is great wisdom in what Semrad has to say. I find, too, that people wrestling with perform-ance addiction have a very difficult time dealing with sadness. They fear that it will slow them down and lead to depression; then they won't be left with the energy to perform. The irony, I have found, is that people who tune in to sadness can allow the emotion to help put their lives into perspective.

Obviously, sadness is not a springboard to higher education or perfecting your skills or mastering new strategies. Rather, it is the fuel that will help you learn how to adapt to change and see the world in different ways. Sadness can help you accept behavior that does not conform to the religion of performance addiction, con-front areas of blindness, and form closer human bonds. Sadness is not depression. It is an emotional cue that allows you to slow down, reflect, absorb disappointment, and move on with renewed focus. In fact, if sadness is not experienced, it can become depression, depleting your energy and ultimately depriving you of important learning opportunities.

Lifelong Learner

Malcolm Knowles, one of the leading experts in adult education, has written about proactive learning—that is, developing the skills that allow for adaptation to change—rather than reactive learning, which is acquiring information passively without developing the means to inquire. Required for proactive learning, Knowles observes, is what psychoanalyst Heinz Kohut called "a cohesive sense of self." That sense of self "allows for internal consistency, in terms of one's identity, while also allowing for reasonable management of anxiety in the face of change. In other words, one has the faith that through initiative, motivation, and competent self-direction, new challenges can be mastered and new learning can be integrated into an ever expanding self."

You can achieve this cohesive sense of self—the power to become a proactive, lifelong learner—by dealing with performance addiction. People who experience the subconscious compulsions of performance addiction—but who do not confront that addiction—are essentially thrown off every time change is introduced. To someone held in the thrall of performance addiction, change is threatening rather than welcome because it is a constant reminder of imperfections and the inability to control outcomes. (People with performance addiction often rant against the messiness of surprises and accidents as well as the enraging inevitability of human failings.)

As I have pointed out in my discussions of perfectionism, this aspect of performance addiction is maladaptive. It is a defense against feelings of inferiority, but it doesn't work. Perfectionism contributes to feelings of contingent self-worth—that is, feelings that your worth is dependent on the approval of other people—rather than the cohesive sense of self that is necessary for proactive learning and adaptive behavior. When self-worth depends exclusively on accomplishment, position, performance, money, or material possessions, then the loss of any of those items erodes the sense of self-worth. Performance addicts depend mostly on all the exterior measurements of value rather than having the interior cohesiveness that makes it possible to accept change. This sets up many of the conditions of loneliness such as poor marriages, remoteness from family and friends, and the fascinations with materialism and image that lead to estrangement.

I think we owe it to ourselves to be lifelong learners not only to maintain meaning in life but also to continue to find wonder in life. Our lives must be continually discovered rather than mastered. In order to learn, you need to understand in the depths of your heart that mistakes are necessary. Making a mistake does not make *you* a mistake.

The misconception that you must escape sadness, avoid mistakes, and strive for accomplishment at all times may be precisely what has caused you pain. Performance addiction is a path leading to fruitless efforts to obtain satisfaction and love. If it remains the driving force in your life, it will most certainly make it impossible for you to feel comfortable in your own skin. Competing, striving, and growing personally and professionally are not negative traits. In fact, it is very important to actualize your talents. But actualizing your potential in various aspects of your life is not synonymous with performance addiction. Once performance addiction takes hold, your potential is impaired rather than enhanced.

As we have seen, the effects of performance addiction permeate every aspect of family, home, and workplace. Everywhere we turn, we are pursued by reminders of its impact on our education, vocation, and relationships. The measures of success and failure, and the judgments about our standing in American society, are omnipresent. No one is free of the struggle.

But we are well equipped to treat ourselves as individuals whom we hold in high regard. If you truly have faith in yourself, your faith will be reflected in the ordinary things that you do on an ongoing basis. Your deeper respect for yourself is evidenced by your ability to take care of yourself and those close to you with consistency. That ability becomes a foundation, and with that foundation you can achieve genuine, healthy accomplishment throughout your lifetime.

What You Can Do about Performance Addiction

Considering what you have learned throughout this book, describe as honestly as possible what you believe constitutes a successful personal and professional life. Where do you stand in relation to your description? What changes will you commit to making to move yourself in the direction of what you consider to be a rich, balanced life? What person closest to you will you share this information with? Be courageous and begin the journey!

Resources

Recommended Reading

Albom, Mitch. *Tuesdays with Morrie: An Old Man, a Young Man, and Life's Greatest Lesson.* New York: Doubleday, 1997.

Braun, Stephen. *The Science of Happiness: Unlocking the Mysteries of Mood.* New York: John Wiley, 2000.

Brody, Howard. *The Placebo Response: How You Can Release the Body's Inner Pharmacy for Better Health.* New York: Harper Collins, 2000.

Ciaramicoli, Arthur, and Katherine Ketcham. *The Power of Empathy: A Practical Guide to Creating Intimacy, Self-Understanding, and Lasting Love.* New York: Plume, 2001.

Cooper, Kenneth. *It's Better to Believe.* Nashville: Thomas Nelson, 1995.

Cox, Harvey. *Common Prayers: Faith, Family, and a Christian's Journey through the Jewish Year.* Boston: Houghton Mifflin, 2001.

Damasio, Antonio. *Descartes' Error: Emotion, Reason, and the Human Brain.* New York: G. P. Putnam's, 1994.

———. *The Feeling of What Happens: Body and Emotions in the Making of Consciousness.* New York: Harcourt Brace and Company, 1999.

Dodes, Lance. *The Heart of Addiction.* New York: Harper Collins, 2002.

Dossey, Larry. *Healing Words.* San Francisco: Harper Collins, 1993.

Effron-Potter, Ron, and Pat Effron-Potter. *Letting Go of Anger: The 10 Most Common Anger Styles and What to Do about Them.* Oakland, Calif.: New Harbinger Publications, 1995.

Forni, P. M. *Choosing Civility: The Twenty-Five Rules of Considerate Conduct.* New York: St. Martin's Press, 2002.

Frankl, Victor. *The Will to Meaning.* New York: Plume, 1969.

Fromm, Erich. *The Art of Loving.* New York: Harper and Row, 1956.

Fumento, Michael. *The Fat of the Land: The Obesity Epidemic and How Overweight Americans Can Help Themselves.* New York: Viking, 1997.

Gibran, Kahil. *Broken Wings.* Trans. Juan Cole. New York: Penguin, 1998.

———. *A Tear and a Smile.* Trans. H. M. Nahmed. New York: Knopf, 1950.

Gleick, James. *Faster: The Acceleration of Just About Everything.* New York: Vintage, 2000.

Goleman, Daniel. *Emotional Intelligence: Why It Can Matter More Than IQ.* New York: Bantam, 1995.

———. *Working with Emotional Intelligence.* New York: Bantam, 1998.

Gottman, John, with Nan Silver. *The Seven Principles for Making Marriage Work: A Practical Guide from the Country's Foremost Relationship Expert.* New York: Three Rivers Press, 1999.

Grayson, Jonathan. *Freedom from Obsessive Compulsive Disorder: A Personalized Recovery Program for Living with Uncertainty.* New York: Jeremy P. Tarcher/Penguin, 2003.

Haas, Elton. *Staying Healthy with Nutrition: The Complete Guide to Diet and Nutritional Medicine.* Berkeley: Celestial Arts, 1993.

Hanh, Thich Nhat. *Living Buddha, Living Christ.* New York: Riverhead Books, 1995.

Horbacher, Marya. *Waisted: A Memoir of Anorexia and Bulimia.* New York: Harper Perennial, 1998.

Kabat-Zinn, Jon. *Wherever You Go There You Are.* New York: Hyperion, 1994.

Kasser, Tim. *The High Price of Materialism.* Cambridge, Mass.: MIT Press, 2002.

Keen, Sam. *To Love and Be Loved.* New York: Bantam, 1997.

Knowles, M., and C. Clevins. *Materials and Methods in Adult and Continuing Education.* Los Angeles: Klevins, 1987.

Lewis, Thomas, Fari Amini, and Richard Lannon. *A General Theory of Love.* New York: Random House, 2000.

Maslow, Abraham. *The Farther Reaches of Human Nature.* New York: Viking, 1971.

Miller, Alice. *The Drama of the Gifted Child: The Search for the True Self.* New York: Basic Books, 1994.

———. *The Untouched Key: Tracing Childhood Trauma in Creativity and Destructivness.* New York: Doubleday, 1990.

Myers, David. *The American Paradox: Hunger in an Age of Plenty.* New Haven, Conn.: Yale University Press, 2000.

Norgay, Jamling Tenzing. *Touching My Father's Soul: A Sherpa's Journey to the Top of Everest.* New York: Harper Collins, 2001.

Ornish, Dean. *Love and Survival: 8 Pathways to Intimacy and Health.* New York: Harper Perennial, 1998.

Pelletier, Kenneth. *Sound Mind—Sound Body.* New York: Simon and Schuster, 1994.

Prather, Hugh. *Notes to Myself: My Struggle to Become a Person.* New York: Bantam, 1983.

Rowe, John, and Robert Kahn. *Successful Aging: The MacArthur Foundation Study Shows You How the Lifestyle Choices You Make Now—More than Heredity—Determine Your Health and Vitality.* New York: Pantheon Books, 1998.

Slaney, Robert B., Kenneth G. Rice, and Jeffrey S. Ashby. "A Programmatic Approach to Measuring Perfectionism: The Almost Perfect Scales." In *Perfectionism: Theory, Research, and Treatment,* ed. Gordon L. Flett and Paul L. Hewitt. Washington, D.C.: American Psychological Association, 2002.

Thayer, Robert. *Calm Energy: How People Regulate Mood with Food and Exercise.* New York: Oxford University Press, 2001.

Washton, Arnold, and Donna Boundy. *Willpower Is Not Enough: Recovering from Addictions of Every Kind.* New York: Perennial, 1990.

Williams, Redford, and Virginia Williams. *Anger Kills: 17 Strategies for Controlling the Hostility that Can Harm Your Health.* New York: Harper Collins, 1993.

Web Sites

American Holistic Health Association
ahha@healthy.net
A comprehensive Web site devoted to all aspects of health, featuring the Medline search engine, which gives access to international articles on health topics.

American Psychological Association
www.apa.org
Features articles that highlight the latest advancements in psychological research on a variety of subjects.

American Society for Addiction Medicine
www.asam.org
Specializes in educating and improving treatment for all addictions.

Anxiety Disorders Association of America
www.adaa.org
Provides access to the latest research findings and treatments of anxiety disorders.

Association for Humanistic Psychology
www.ahpweb.org
Provides access to relevant journals, bibliographies, and related Web sites.

Health Emotions Research Institute
www.healthemotions.org
Accents how positive emotions influence the body, prevent disease, and increase overall resiliency.

Internet Mental Health
www.mentalhealth.com
Comprehensive information on a variety of mental disorders.

Obsessive Compulsive Foundation
www.ocfoundation.org
Provides current information about the treatment of obsessive-compulsive disorder, as well as information about support groups throughout the world.

Research Matters (Harvard Medical School)
www.researchmatters.harvard.edu
Explores state-of-the-art Harvard research findings in the areas of
  mind, body, and society.

Newsletters

Blues Buster: The Newsletter about Depression
P.O. Box 52021
Boulder, CO 80321-2021
A plainly written newsletter with interesting articles about the ori-
  gins of depression. The editors discuss recent treatment strategies
  and effective suggestions to help people begin coping differently.
  They accent the interpersonal aspect of depression, as well as
  featuring articles on the nutritional component of low moods.

Harvard Mental Health Letter
P.O. Box 420448
Palm Coast, FL 32141-0448
An excellent resource dealing with all areas of mental health. This
  letter provides updates from the leading clinicians and theoreti-
  cians in the United States. It is written in a practical, easy-to-
  understand style.

Tufts University Health and Nutrition Letter
P.O. Box 420235
Palm Coast, FL 32142-0235
The Tufts newsletter addresses all aspects of health, featuring
  experts from one of the leading nutrition schools in the United
  States. This clearly written letter discusses the latest develop-
  ments in maintaining comprehensive health.

University of California, Berkeley, Wellness Letter
P.O. Box 420148
Palm Coast, FL 32142
An exceptional newsletter addressing media coverage of nutrition,
  fitness, and self-care. This newsletter is recommended for anyone
  who is interested in the most recent definitive findings on health
  topics.

Index